797,885 Books
are available to read at

www.ForgottenBooks.com

Forgotten Books' App
Available for mobile, tablet & eReader

ISBN 978-1-332-73335-4
PIBN 10280608

This book is a reproduction of an important historical work. Forgotten Books uses state-of-the-art technology to digitally reconstruct the work, preserving the original format whilst repairing imperfections present in the aged copy. In rare cases, an imperfection in the original, such as a blemish or missing page, may be replicated in our edition. We do, however, repair the vast majority of imperfections successfully; any imperfections that remain are intentionally left to preserve the state of such historical works.

Forgotten Books is a registered trademark of FB &c Ltd.
Copyright © 2015 FB &c Ltd.
FB &c Ltd, Dalton House, 60 Windsor Avenue, London, SW19 2RR.
Company number 08720141. Registered in England and Wales.

For support please visit www.forgottenbooks.com

1 MONTH OF FREE READING

at
www.ForgottenBooks.com

By purchasing this book you are eligible for one month membership to ForgottenBooks.com, giving you unlimited access to our entire collection of over 700,000 titles via our web site and mobile apps.

To claim your free month visit:
www.forgottenbooks.com/free280608

* Offer is valid for 45 days from date of purchase. Terms and conditions apply.

English
Français
Deutsche
Italiano
Español
Português

www.forgottenbooks.com

Mythology Photography **Fiction**
Fishing Christianity **Art** Cooking
Essays Buddhism Freemasonry
Medicine **Biology** Music **Ancient Egypt** Evolution Carpentry Physics
Dance Geology **Mathematics** Fitness
Shakespeare **Folklore** Yoga Marketing
Confidence Immortality Biographies
Poetry **Psychology** Witchcraft
Electronics Chemistry History **Law**
Accounting **Philosophy** Anthropology
Alchemy Drama Quantum Mechanics
Atheism Sexual Health **Ancient History**
Entrepreneurship Languages Sport
Paleontology Needlework Islam
Metaphysics Investment Archaeology
Parenting Statistics Criminology
Motivational

W. H. **WHEELER'S**

GRADED STUDIES

IN

GREAT AUTHORS

A COMPLETE SPELLER

A BOOK WHICH HATH BEEN CULLED FROM THE FLOWERS
OF ALL BOOKS. — *George Eliot.*

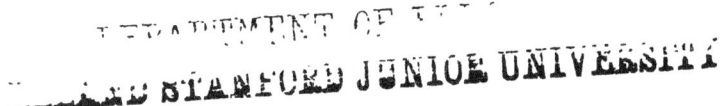

CHICAGO
W. H. WHEELER & COMPANY

551282

COPYRIGHT, 1899, BY

W. H. WHEELER.

TYPOGRAPHY BY J. S. CUSHING & CO., NORWOOD, MASS.

ENGRAVINGS AND PRINTING BY ROGERS & WELLS, CHICAGO.

PREFACE.

Of all the alphabetic languages English is said to be the most difficult to spell. In a perfect language each letter always has the same sound, and each sound is always represented by the same letter; but in English *a* represents a different sound in each of the words *hate, hat, far, all, ask, care, many, what,* and so with other letters. A single sound may be represented by many different characters. Thus the sound of *a* as in *hate* is represented by different characters in each of the words *faint, play, eight, they, great, gauge,* and so with other sounds. In a perfect language there are no words pronounced alike and spelled two or three different ways; but in English there are hundreds of such words.

A thorough reform of this "monstrous English spelling" is in progress, and will prove a priceless boon to countless millions yet unborn, but the children now in school must be taught to spell according to the present standard. The more difficult it is to learn it, the more necessary it is to teach it. Inability to spell correctly is always considered an indication of a lack of culture, although the complaints from our universities, our colleges, our high schools, the press, and the school patrons all indicate that good spelling is rare.

In the preparation of "Graded Studies in Great Authors" the author was guided by the conviction that whatever we wish a child to learn for future use must be attractively presented, and that the child's mind should be early stored with beautiful and vital truths expressed in choicest language. He first selected a vocabulary which fairly represents the peculiarities of English spelling, and then searched literature for choice sentences which illustrate the use of these words. It is conceded that for a child the best knowledge of a word is to know it as used in a memorable sentence by one of the great masters of expression.

As the child is likely to carry through life what is copied or repeated from school books, the illustrative sentences should present the richest thoughts and choicest gems of expression that can be gathered from literature. In these rambles with the poets the child will hear the carol of the lark, the babbling of the brook, and the music of the sea; he will see the rainbow's arch, the sumac's gold and red, and the sunshine and the shadow chasing each other over the billowy fields. The child who is led into the bypaths of nature by these great word painters will learn to look through all "the five windows of the soul"; he will be charmed with the beauty of his surroundings; he will be deeply impressed with the dignity, power, and beauty of our mother tongue, the richest of all languages; he will be inspired to put meaning into his own sentences; he will learn that it is the gift of poetry to hallow every place in which it moves,— to breathe round nature a fragrance more exquisite than the perfume of the rose, and to shed over it a tint more magical than the blush of the morning.

Pupils will like to know about the authors of the selections, and will easily remember their names, their dates, their most famous works, some traits of their characters and incidents of

PREFACE.

their lives. Learning these in connection with each selection will be good preparation for the study of the history of literature. Do not speak of the personal deformities or failings of these great masters of literature. Do not ask the child to change poetry into prose. Teach him rather that a beautiful poem or a piece of noble prose is a work of art, and that he has no more right to change it or mar it than he has to mar a beautiful statue or a fine painting. These gems of thought and flowers of fancy have been gathered from many sources. In collecting them the author has wandered far through the flowery paths of literature; and, while the search has been a long one, he is loth to come to the end of a journey so enchanting.

In the preparation of these lessons the author has received suggestions from many teachers, to whom he gratefully acknowledges his indebtedness. He also takes pleasure in acknowledging his great indebtedness to his critic, the eminent philologist, Dr. Francis A. March of Lafayette College. Acknowledgments are due to Houghton, Mifflin & Co., and G. P. Putnam's Sons, for permission to use selections from their publications.

AMENDED SPELLING.

The following rule for amended spelling is drawn from the usage of the greatest poets, and recommended by the Philological Societies of England and America: —

    Rule. When final *ed* is pronounced as *t*, spell it with *t*.

1. Night's candles are *burnt* out, and jocund day
   Stands tiptoe on the misty mountain tops.
   — WILLIAM SHAKESPEARE.

2. I hope to meet my Pilot face to face,
   When I have *crost* the bar. — ALFRED TENNYSON.

3.   Having gathered flowers,
   Stript the beds and *spoilt* the bowers. — ROBERT BROWNING.

4. Though old the thought, and oft *exprest*,
   'Tis his at last who says it best. — JAMES RUSSELL LOWELL.

5. And silver white the river gleams,
   As if Diana, in her dreams,
   Had *dropt* her silver bow
   Upon the meadows low. — HENRY WADSWORTH LONGFELLOW.

The National Educational Association has adopted the following simplified spellings: —

tho	for though	program	for programme	prolog	for prologue
thru	" through	thruout	" throughout	demagog	" demagogue
altho	" although	thorofare	" thoroughfare	decalog	" decalogue
thoro	" thorough	catalog	" catalogue	pedagog	" pedagogue

GRADED STUDIES IN GREAT AUTHORS.

LESSON 1.

Long a as in hate, marked ā.

1. Copy the following sentences. Note carefully the capital letters and punctuation. 2. Write from dictation.

1. Better three hours too soon than a minute too *late*.
 —WILLIAM SHAKESPEARE.
2. She seemed as happy as a *wave*
 That dances on the sea.—WILLIAM WORDSWORTH.

3. How cool was the shadow the long branches *gave*,
 As they hung from the willow, and dipp'd in the *wave*.
 —AMELIA B. WELBY.
4. And all the beauty of the *place*
 Is in thy heart and on thy *face*.
 —WILLIAM CULLEN BRYANT.
5. Hear the dewy echoes calling
 From *cave* to *cave!*—ALFRED TENNYSON.

6. The queen of the spring, as she passed down the *vale*,
 Left her robe in the trees and her breath in the *gale*.
 —JOHN HOLLAND.
7. With spiders I had friendship *made*,
 And watch'd them in their sullen *trade*.
 —GEORGE GORDON, LORD BYRON.

LESSON 2.

āi = a long, marked a.

1. Copy the following sentences. Note carefully the capital letters, punctuation, and rhyme. 2. Write from dictation.

1. *Aim* at the highest. — JOHN MILTON.

2. Wise men ne'er sit and *wail* their loss.
— WILLIAM SHAKESPEARE.

3. They never *fail* who die in a great cause.
— GEORGE GORDON, LORD BYRON.

4. And just a quiet country lane,
Fringed close by fields of grass and *grain,*
Was the crooked road that crossed the *plain.*
— PHŒBE CARY.

5. The selfish heart deserves the *pain* it feels.
EDWARD YOUNG.

6. They never sought in *vain,* that sought the Lord aright! — ROBERT BURNS.

7. Sleep came at length, but with a *train*
Of feelings true and fancies *vain.* — SIR WALTER SCOTT.

8. Low lispings of the summer *rain,*
Dropping on the ripened *grain.*
— HENRY WADSWORTH LONGFELLOW.

9.   The soft hues
That *stain* the wild bird's wing, and flush the clouds.
— HENRY WADSWORTH LONGFELLOW.

10. The *maiden* Spring upon the *plain*
Came in a sun-lit fall of *rain.* — ALFRED TENNYSON.

LESSON 3.

āy = a long, marked ā.

1. Copy the following sentences carefully. Remember that the punctuation is a part of the written sentence. 2. Write from dictation.

1. And on the *bay* the moonlight *lay*,
   And the shadow of the moon.
   —SAMUEL TAYLOR COLERIDGE.

2. Again the sunny month of *May*
   Has made our hills and valleys *gay*. — ROBERT BURNS.

3. Maud Muller on a summer's *day*,
   Raked the meadows sweet with *hay*.
   — JOHN GREENLEAF WHITTIER.

4.   Until the break of *day*
   Through this house each fairy *stray*.
   — WILLIAM SHAKESPEARE.

5. I see them on their winding *way;*
   Above their ranks the moonbeams *play*.
   — REGINALD HEBER.

6. Hear how the birds, on ev'ry blooming *spray*,
   With joyous music wake the dawning *day!*
   —ALEXANDER POPE.

7. "Come up! come up!" They seem to *say*,
   "Where the topmost twigs in the breezes *sway*."
   —MARY HOWITT.

8. See yon *gay* goldfinch hop from *spray* to *spray*,
   Who sings a farewell to the parting *day*. — JOHN GAY.

LESSON 4.

Review.

1. Copy the following sentences. Underscore all the words containing ā, āi, or āy. 2. Write from dictation.

1. While misty dawn, and moonbeam pale,
   Still mingled in the silent dale. — Sir Walter Scott.

2. O stay, sweet warbling wood-lark, stay,
   Nor quit for me the trembling spray. — Robert Burns.

3.   Where Nature never gave
   A brook to murmur or a bough to wave.
                        William Wordsworth.

4. Here hath been dawning another blue day;
   Think, wilt thou let it slip useless away?
                       — Thomas Carlyle.

5. And how should the hills be clothed with grain,
   The vales with flowers be crowned,
   But for the chain of silver rain
   That draws them out of the ground. — Alice Cary.

6. Look up! The wide extended plain
   Is billowy with its ripened grain.
                   — William Henry Burleigh.

7.   But they fade,
   The mist and the river, the hill and the shade.
                     — William Wordsworth.

8. There, all around, the gentlest breezes stray;
   There gentle music melts on ev'ry spray.
                     — Oliver Goldsmith.

LESSON 5.

Short a as in hat, marked ă.

1. Copy the following sentences. Note carefully the punctuation. 2. Write from dictation.

1. The wild birds *sang*, the echoes *rang*. — ROBERT BURNS.

2.   The ocean rolls
Its broad, bright surges to the sloping *sand*.
— PERCY BYSSHE SHELLEY.

3. Now, o'er the earth a solemn stillness *ran*,
And lull'd alike the cares of brute and *man*.
— GEORGE GORDON, LORD BYRON.

4. Among the lilacs *hand* in *hand*,
And two by two in fairy *land*.
— ROBERT LOUIS STEVENSON.

5. Here Ceres'[1] gifts in waving prospect *stand*,
And nodding tempt the joyful reaper's *hand*.
— ALEXANDER POPE.

6. Twilight brought *back* the evening star to the sky.
HENRY WADSWORTH LONGFELLOW.

7. *Land* of my sires! what mortal *hand*
Can e'er untie the filial *band*
That knits me to thy rugged *strand*!
— SIR WALTER SCOTT.

8. Love took up the glass of Time, *and* turn'd it in his glowing *hands*;
Every moment, lightly shaken, *ran* itself in golden *sands*. — ALFRED TENNYSON.

---

[1] Ce′res, the goddess of corn and harvests.

LESSON 6.

Long e as in me, marked ē. ēe = ē.

1. Copy the following sentences carefully. 2. Write from dictation.

1. If *she be* not so to *me,*
   What care I how fair *she be?* — GEORGE WITHER.

2. *We* cannot *be here* and there too.
   — WILLIAM SHAKESPEARE.

3. *She* sings it under our own *green tree,*
   To the babe half slumbering on her *knee.*
   FELICIA D. HEMANS.

4. I *feed* the clouds, the rainbows, and the flowers.
   PERCY BYSSHE SHELLEY.

5. Dewdrops are the gems of morning,
   But the tears of mournful *eve.*
   — SAMUEL TAYLOR COLERIDGE.

6. All the broad leaves over *me*
   Clap their little hands in *glee.*
   HENRY WADSWORTH LONGFELLOW.

7. A calm, unbroken *sleep*
   Is on the blue waves of the *deep.* — GEORGE D. PRENTICE.

8. The feathered people you might *see,*
   Perched all around on every *tree.* — ROBERT BURNS.

9. Now night grows *deep,*
   And silent as its clouds, and full of *sleep.*
   FELICIA D. HEMANS.

LESSON 7.

ee = e long, marked ē.

1. Copy the following sentences carefully. 2. Write from dictation.

1. Mildly and soft the western *breeze*
   Just kiss'd the lake, just stirr'd the *trees.*
   — Sir Walter Scott.

2. Honor to those whose words and *deeds*
   Thus help us in our daily *needs.*
   — Henry Wadsworth Longfellow.

3. Blossom of the almond *trees,*
   April's gift to April's *bees.* — Edwin Arnold.

4. Sunbeam! what gift has the world like *thee?*
   — Felicia D. Hemans.

5. How pleasant the life of a bird must be,
   Flitting about in a leafy *tree!* — Mary Howitt.

6. Here are cool mosses *deep,*
   And thro' the moss the ivies *creep.* — Alfred Tennyson.

7. Kindling a flush on the fair *cheek* of spring.
   — Percy Bysshe Shelley.

8. But *sleep* stole on, as *sleep* will do
   When hearts are light and life is new.
   — John Greenleaf Whittier.

9. And her sunny locks
   Hang on her temples like a golden *fleece.*
   — William Shakespeare.

LESSON 8.

ēa = e long, marked ē.

1. Copy the following sentences carefully. 2. Write from dictation.

1. Touch us gently, Time!
   Let us glide adown thy *stream*
   Gently,— as we sometimes glide
   Through a quiet *dream*.— BRYAN WALLER PROCTER.

2. The same sweet sounds are in my *ear*
   My early childhood loved to *hear*.
   — WILLIAM CULLEN BRYANT.

3. Who rowing hard against the *stream*,
   Saw distant gates of Eden *gleam*,
   And did not *dream* it was a *dream*.— ALFRED TENNYSON.

4. Our bread was such as captives' *tears*
   Have moisten'd many a thousand *years*.
   — GEORGE GORDON, LORD BYRON.

5. Hark! the numbers soft and *clear*
   Gently *steal* upon the *ear*.— ALEXANDER POPE.

6. Under the snowdrifts the blossoms are sleeping,
   Dreaming their *dreams* of sunshine and June.
   HARRIET PRESCOTT SPOFFORD.

7. My heart *leaps* up when I behold a rainbow in the sky.
   — WILLIAM WORDSWORTH.

8. Those silver sounds, so soft, so *dear*,
   The listener held his breath to *hear*.— SIR WALTER SCOTT.

LESSON 9.
Review.

1. Copy the following sentences. Underscore all the words containing ē, ēe, or ēa.   2. Write from dictation.

1.   Songsters of the early year
Are every day more sweet to hear. — Robert Burns.

2. This new life is likely to be
Hard for a gay young fellow like me.
                              William Cullen Bryant.

3. Not the faintest motion could be seen
Of all the shades that slanted o'er the green.
                                       John Keats.

4. So soft, though high, so loud, and yet so clear,
Even listening angels lean'd from heaven to hear.
                                     — Alexander Pope.

5. Now spring has clad the grove in green,
And strew'd the lea with flowers. — Robert Burns.

6. For bright as brightest sunshine
The light of memory streams
Round the old-fashioned homestead,
Where I dreamed my dream of dreams! — Alice Cary.

7. And Nature, the old nurse, took
The child upon her knee,
Saying · "Here is a story book
Thy Father has written for thee."
                                 — Henry Wadsworth Longfellow.

LESSON 10.

Short e as in met, marked ĕ.

1. Copy the following sentences carefully.   2. Write from dictation.

1. The young girl mused beside the *well*,
   Till the rain on the unraked clover *fell*.
   JOHN GREENLEAF WHITTIER.

2. *When* the *red* tints of the *west*
   Prove the sun is gone to *rest*. — KARL HERRLOSSOHN.

3. *Violets* are gone from their grassy *dell*,
   With the cowslip cups, where the fairies *dwell*.
   — FELICIA D. HEMANS.

4. A name which you all know by sight *very well*,
   But which no one can speak, and no one can *spell*.
   ROBERT SOUTHEY.

5. A rose-lipped *shell* that murmured of the eternal sea.
   JOSIAH GILBERT HOLLAND.

6. With a bee in *every bell*,
   Almond bloom, we greet thee *well*. — EDWIN ARNOLD.

7. O'er me, like a regal *tent*,
   Cloudy-ribbed, the *sunset bent*.
   — JOHN GREENLEAF WHITTIER.

8. *Yes*, sweet it seems across some watery *dell*
   To catch the music of the pealing *bell*.
   — REGINALD HEBER.

9. No bird so wild but has its *quiet nest*.
   PERCY BYSSHE SHELLEY.

JOHN MILTON

1608 ⁂ 1674

LESSON 11.
Review.

1. Copy the following sentences. Underscore all the words containing ă or ŏ. 2. Write from dictation.

1. For youth loves not the things that are sad,
    But turns to the hopeful and the glad. — PHŒBE CARY.

2.   Behind the black wall of the forest,
    Tipping its summit with silver, arose the moon.
    — HENRY WADSWORTH LONGFELLOW.

3. Far in the chambers of the west,
    The gale had sigh'd itself to rest. — SIR WALTER SCOTT.

4. Freedom, hand in hand with labor,
    Walketh strong and brave. — JOHN GREENLEAF WHITTIER.

5. And on their way, in friendly chat,
    Now talked of this, and then of that. — JAMES MERRICK.

6. It is well to think well. It is divine to act well.
    HORACE MANN.

7. Fine sense and exalted sense are not half so useful as common sense. — ALEXANDER POPE.

8. Blue were her eyes as the fairy flax,
    Her cheeks like the dawn of day.
    HENRY WADSWORTH LONGFELLOW.

9. Thy looks, thy gestures, all present
    The picture of a life well spent.
    — WILLIAM WORDSWORTH.

LESSON 11.

Review.

1. Copy the following sentences. Underscore all the words containing ă or ŏ. 2. Write from dictation.

1. For youth loves not the things that are sad,
   But turns to the hopeful and the glad. — PHŒBE CARY.

2.   Behind the black wall of the forest,
   Tipping its summit with silver, arose the moon.
                           —HENRY WADSWORTH LONGFELLOW.

3. Far in the chambers of the west,
   The gale had sigh'd itself to rest. — SIR WALTER SCOTT.

4. Freedom, hand in hand with labor,
   Walketh strong and brave. — JOHN GREENLEAF WHITTIER.

5. And on their way, in friendly chat,
   Now talked of this, and then of that. — JAMES MERRICK.

6. It is well to think well. It is divine to act well.
                           — HORACE MANN.

7. Fine sense and exalted sense are not half so useful
   as common sense. — ALEXANDER POPE.

8. Blue were her eyes as the fairy flax,
   Her cheeks like the dawn of day.
                      HENRY WADSWORTH LONGFELLOW.

9. Thy looks, thy gestures, all present
   The picture of a life well spent.
                           —WILLIAM WORDSWORTH.

LESSON 12.

Hard c as in **can** = **k**, marked **c**.

1. Copy the following sentences carefully. 2. Write from dictation.

1. Then *catch* the moments as they fly.—ROBERT BURNS.

2. Sing away, aye, sing away,
   Merry little bird,
   Though your life from youth to age
   Passes in a narrow *cage*.—DINAH MARIA MULOCK.

3. My *crown* is *called content;*
   A *crown* it is that seldom kings enjoy.
   —WILLIAM SHAKESPEARE.

4. He that keeps nor *crust* nor *crumb*,
   Weary of all, shall want some.—WILLIAM SHAKESPEARE.

5. Yon *clear* spring tells no tale
   Of all the good it's done.—WILLIAM CULLEN BRYANT.

6. The rainbow hangs on the poising wave,
   And sweet is the *color* of *cove* and *cave*.
   —ALFRED TENNYSON.

7. And I think of the smiling faces
   That used to watch and wait,
   Till the *click* of the *clock* was answered
   By the *click* of the opening gate.
   —JAMES WHITCOMB RILEY.

8. Sweet day, so *cool*, so *calm*, so bright.
   —GEORGE HERBERT.

LESSON 13.

Soft **c** as in **ice**, marked ç = s.

1. Copy the following sentences carefully. 2. Write from dictation.

1. The *price* of wisdom is above rubies. — BIBLE.

2. Winter creeps along with tardy *pace*,
   Sour is his front, and furrow'd is his *face*.
   —JOHN DRYDEN.

3. Dreaming upon the wonderful sweet *face*
   Of Nature, in a wild and pathless *place*.
   — FREDERICK TENNYSON.

4. The tender *grace* of a day that is dead
   Will never come back to me. — ALFRED TENNYSON.

5.   Envious streaks
   Do *lace* the severing clouds in yonder east.
   — WILLIAM SHAKESPEARE.

6. Free as the wind, or feathered *race*
   That hop from spray to spray. — ROBERT BURNS.

7. And thou, vast Ocean! on whose awful *face*
   Time's iron feet can print no *trace*.
   — ROBERT MONTGOMERY.

8. O *city* of the seven proud hills!
   Whose name e'en yet the spirit thrills.
   —FELICIA D. HEMANS.

9. Pure gurgling rills the lonely desert *trace*
   And waste their music on the savage *race*.
   — EDWARD YOUNG.

LESSON 14.

Long i as in pine, marked ī.

1. Copy the following sentences carefully. 2. Write from dictation.

1. Her lips are *like* the cherries *ripe*. — ROBERT BURNS.

2. Alone, alone, all, all alone,
   Alone on the *wide, wide* sea!
   — SAMUEL TAYLOR COLERIDGE.

3. The green trees whispered low and *mild;*
   They were my playmates when a *child,*
   And rocked me in their arms so *wild!*
   HENRY WADSWORTH LONGFELLOW.

4. Vain, very vain my weary search to *find*
   That bliss which only centers in the *mind.*
   OLIVER GOLDSMITH.

5. *Like* one who *spies,* or thinks he *spies,*
   Through flickering clouds the new moon *rise.* — VIRGIL.

6. Each purple peak, each flinty *spire,*
   Was bathed in floods of living *fire.* — SIR WALTER SCOTT.

7. To hear the lark begin his *flight,*
   And singing startle the dull *Night,*
   From his watch-tower in the *skies,*
   Till the dappled dawn doth *rise.* — JOHN MILTON.

8. *While* to the music, from on *high,*
   The echoes make a glad reply. — WILLIAM WORDSWORTH.

LESSON 15.

ỹ = i long, marked ĭ.

1. Copy the following sentences carefully. 2. Write from dictation.

1. In and out like arrows *fly*
   The slender swallows, swift and *shy*. — Phœbe Cary.

2. Oh! lagging hours, how slow you *fly!*
   — Percy Bysshe Shelley.

3. A brood of nature's minstrels chirp and *fly*,
   Glad as the sunshine and the laughing *sky*.
   — John Clare.

4. The tear, down childhood's cheek that flows,
   Is like the dewdrop on the rose;
   When next the summer breeze comes *by*
   And waves the bush, the flower is *dry*.
   — Sir Walter Scott.

5. When the bloom was on the clover, and the blue
     was in the *sky*,
   And my happy heart brimmed over in the days gone
     by. — James Whitcomb Riley.

6. "Will you walk into my parlor?"
     Said the spider to the *fly*.
   "'Tis the prettiest little parlor
     That ever you did *spy*." — Mary Howitt.

7. Blow, bugle, blow, set the wild echoes *flying*,
   And answer, echoes, answer, *dying, dying, dying*.
   — Alfred Tennyson.

LESSON 16.

Review.

1. Copy the following sentences. Underscore all the words containing ī or ȳ. 2. Write from dictation.

1. Out of the shadow of night,
   The world rolls into light.
   —Henry Wadsworth Longfellow.

2. As a violet's gentle eye
   Gazes on the azure sky.—Percy Bysshe Shelley.

3. Tell me, fellow-creatures, why
   At my presence thus you fly.—Robert Burns.

4. 'Tis softer than the west wind's sigh.
   Percy Bysshe Shelley.

5. Let dimpled Mirth his temples twine
   With tendrils of the laughing vine.
   —Sir Walter Scott.

6. Alone, in that dark sorrow, hour after hour crept by;
   Star after star looked palely in and sank adown the sky.—John Greenleaf Whittier.

7. If I'm not so large as you,
   You are not so small as I,
   And not half so spry.—Ralph Waldo Emerson.

8. For 'tis a truth well known to most,
   That whatsoever thing is lost,
   We seek it, ere it come to light,
   In every cranny but the right.—William Cowper.

LESSON 17.

Short ĭ as in **pin**, marked ĭ

1. Copy the following sentences carefully. 2. Write from dictation.

1. Take not away the life you cannot *give;*
   For all *things* have an equal right to *live.*
   — JOHN DRYDEN.

2. To seek the *primrose* where *it springs;*
   Or chase the fly *with* painted *wings.*
   — FELICIA D. HEMANS.

3. Flowers of the field *with* petals *thin,*
   Lilies that neither toil nor *spin.*
   — HENRY WADSWORTH LONGFELLOW.

4. *If* you look to vale or *hill,*
   If you *listen,* all *is still,*
   Save a *little* neighbor*ing rill.* — WILLIAM WORDSWORTH.

5. All was *still,* save that the *hill*
   Was *telling* of the sound. — SAMUEL TAYLOR COLERIDGE.

6. The *insect*-youth are on the *wing,*
   Eager to taste the honeyed *spring.* — THOMAS GRAY.

7. My ears *with tingling* echoes *ring,*
   And life *itself is* on the *wing.*
   — GEORGE GORDON, LORD BYRON.

8. We grant, although he had much *wit,*
   He was very shy of *using it.* — SAMUEL BUTLER.

9. The bee that at her flowery work doth *sing.*
   — JOHN MILTON.

LESSON 18.

1. Copy carefully. 2. Write from dictation, or from memory.

The storybooks have told you
  Of the fairy-folks so nice,
That make them leathern aprons
  Of the ears of little mice;
And wear the leaves of roses,
  Like a cap upon their heads,
And sleep at night on thistle-down,
  Instead of feather beds!

These stories, too, have told you,
  No doubt to your surprise,
That the fairies ride in coaches
  That are drawn by butterflies;
And come into your chambers,
  When you are locked in dreams,
And right across your counterpanes
  Make bold to drive their teams;

* * *

There are no fairy-folk that ride
  About the world at night,
Who give you rings and other things,
  To pay for doing right.
But if you do to others what
  You'd have them do to you,
You'll be as blest as if the best
  Of storybooks were true. — ALICE CARY.

LESSON 19.

Long **o** as in **note**, marked ō.

1. Copy the following sentences carefully. 2. Write from dictation.

1. The leaf is *growing old*,
   And wears in grace of duty done,
   The *gold* and scarlet of the sun.
   — MARGARET E. SANGSTER.

2. The airs and streams renew their joyous *tone*.
   PERCY BYSSHE SHELLEY.

3. Summer gathers up her *robes* of *glory*,
   And like a dream of beauty glides away.
   — SARAH HELEN WHITMAN.

4. The linnet's warble, sinking *toward* a *close*,
   Hints to the thrush 'tis time for their *repose*.
   WILLIAM WORDSWORTH.

5. Time passed, and Autumn came to *fold*
   Green summer in her brown and *gold*.
   JOHN GREENLEAF WHITTIER.

6. The drying up a single tear has *more*
   Of honest fame, than shedding seas of *gore*.
   — GEORGE GORDON, LORD BYRON.

7. Her cap of velvet could not *hold*
   The tresses of her hair of *gold*.
   — HENRY WADSWORTH LONGFELLOW.

8. The morning sets her *rosy* clouds
      Like hedges in the sky,
   And *o'er* and *o'er* their dear *old* tunes
      The winds of evening try. — ALICE CARY.

LESSON 20.

ōa = o long, marked ō.

1. Copy the following sentences carefully. 2. Write from dictation.

1. On one side is a field of drooping *oats*,
   Through which the poppies show their scarlet *coats*.
   JOHN KEATS.

2. Such is the patriot's *boast*, where'er we *roam*,
   His first, best country ever is at home.
   — OLIVER GOLDSMITH.

3. Made white with *foam* the green and purple sea.
   — PERCY BYSSHE SHELLEY.

4. How sweetly did they *float* upon the wings
   Of silence! — JOHN MILTON.

5. Telling tales of the fairy, who traveled like steam,
   In a pumpkin-shell *coach*, with two rats for a team.
   — JOHN GREENLEAF WHITTIER.

6. His great fires up the chimney *roared*;
   The stranger feasted at his *board*.
   — HENRY WADSWORTH LONGFELLOW.

7. 'Tis a bird I love with its brooding note,
   And the trembling throb in its mottled *throat*.
   — NATHANIEL P. WILLIS.

8. Faintly as tolls the evening chime,
   Our voices keep tune and our *oars* keep time.
   — THOMAS MOORE.

9. And when he caught the thrush's note,
   He, too, began to tune his *throat*. — PHŒBE CARY.

LESSON 21.

ōw or ōu = o long, marked ō.

1. Copy the following sentences carefully. 2. Write from dictation.

1. A spring there is, whose silver waters *show*
   Clear as a glass the shining sands *below*.
   ALEXANDER POPE.

2. O look! the sun begins to rise, the heavens are in a *glow;*
   He shines upon a hundred fields, and all of them I *know.* — ALFRED TENNYSON.

3. A thousand feet in depth *below*
   Its massy waters meet and *flow*.
   GEORGE GORDON, LORD BYRON.

4. The singing chimney chanted *low*
   The homely song of long ago.
   — HENRY WADSWORTH LONGFELLOW.

5. The birds *pour* forth their *souls* in notes.
   — WILLIAM WORDSWORTH.

6. *Blow* high, *blow low,* not all its *snow*
   Could quench our hearth-fire's ruddy *glow*.
   JOHN GREENLEAF WHITTIER.

7. Miles and miles of golden green,
   Where the sunflowers *blow*
   In a solid *glow.* — ROBERT BROWNING.

8. Lo! sifted through the winds that *blow,*
   Down comes the soft and silent *snow.*
   — GEORGE W. BUNGAY.

9. And all the echoes *mourn.* — JOHN MILTON.

LESSON 22.

Review.

1. Copy the following sentences. Underscore all the words containing **ō, ōa, ōu,** or **ōw**. 2. Write from dictation.

1. O stretch thy reign, fair Peace! from shore to shore,
   Till conquest cease, and slavery be no more.
   — ALEXANDER POPE.

2. How pleasant thy banks and green valleys below,
   Where wild in the woodlands the primroses blow!
   — ROBERT BURNS.

3. And it mottled the water with amber and gold,
   Till the glad lilies rocked in the ripples that rolled.
   — JAMES WHITCOMB RILEY.

4. We lay beneath a spreading oak,
   Beside a mossy seat;
   And from the turf a fountain broke,
   And gurgled at our feet. — WILLIAM WORDSWORTH.

5. I know the morning; and I love it, fresh and sweet as it is. — DANIEL WEBSTER.

6. O yet we trust that somehow good
   Will be the final goal of ill. — ALFRED TENNYSON.

7. Here the bright crocus and blue violet glow;
   Here western winds on breathing roses blow.
   — ALEXANDER POPE.

8. The course of Nature is the art of God.
   — EDWARD YOUNG.

9. The royal kingcup bold
   Dares not don his coat of gold. — EDWIN ARNOLD.

LESSON 23.

Short o as in not, marked ŏ.

1. Copy the following sentences carefully. 2. Write from dictation.

1. Now the heart is so full that a *drop* overfills it,
   We are happy now because *God* wills it.
   — JAMES RUSSELL LOWELL.

2. The ship was cheered, the harbor cleared;
   Merrily did we *drop*
   Below the kirk, below the hill,
   Below the lighthouse *top*. — SAMUEL TAYLOR COLERIDGE.

3. Well, you have seen it — a tempting *spot!*
   Now come with me through the orchard *plot*
   And down the lane to the gardener's *cot*. — PHŒBE CARY.

4. Spring there shall dress a sweeter *sod*
   Than Fancy's feet have ever *trod*. — WILLIAM COLLINS.

5. So blue *yon* winding river flows,
   It seems an outlet from the sky.
   — HENRY WADSWORTH LONGFELLOW.

6.   Time, that aged nurse,
   Rock'd me to patience. — JOHN KEATS.

7. And lo! as through the western pines,
   On meadow, stream, and *pond*,
   Flamed the red radiance of a sky,
   Set all afire *beyond*. — JOHN GREENLEAF WHITTIER.

LESSON 24.

Review.

1. Copy the following sentences. Underscore all the words containing ĭ or ŏ. 2. Write from dictation.

1. I shot an arrow into the air,
   It fell to earth I knew not where.
   — Henry Wadsworth Longfellow.

2. He that complies against his will,
   Is of his own opinion still. — Samuel Butler.

3. All seem'd as peaceful and as still,
   As the mist slumbering on yon hill.
   — Sir Walter Scott.

4. The voice of the night bird, that sends a thrill
   To the heart of the leaves, when the winds are still.
   — Felicia D. Hemans.

5. The lazy mist hangs from the brow of the hill.
   Robert Burns.

6. Heap on more wood! The wind is chill;
   But, let it whistle as it will,
   We'll keep our merry Christmas still.
   Sir Walter Scott.

7. And some, their very names forgot,
   Not even a stone to mark the spot,
   Yet sleep in peace; so it matters not. — Phœbe Cary.

8. A lovely bird with azure wings,
   And song that said a thousand things,
   And seem'd to say them all for me.
   — George Gordon, Lord Byron.

LESSON 25.

Soft **g** as in **gem**, marked *g*.

1. Copy the following sentences carefully. 2. Write from dictation.

1. All things must *change*
   To something new, to something *strange*.
   — HENRY WADSWORTH LONGFELLOW.

2. Just in the green top of a *hedge*
   That runs along a valley's *edge*
   One star has thrust a golden *wedge*. — ALICE CARY.

3. I find the doctors and the *sages*
   Have differed in all climes and *ages*. — THOMAS MOORE.

4. Ask why God made the *gem* so small,
   While *huge* he made the granite. — ROBERT BURNS.

5. *Change* is the diet upon which all subsist.
   — WILLIAM COWPER.

6. O teach him, while your lessons last,
   To *judge* the present by the past. — SIR WALTER SCOTT.

7. Just at the *age* 'twixt boy and youth,
   When thought is speech, and speech is truth.
   SIR WALTER SCOTT.

8. Skirting the rocks at the forest *edge*
   With a running flame from *ledge* to *ledge*.
   ELAINE GOODALE.

9. In the stream the long-leaved flowers weep,
   And from the craggy *ledge* the poppy hangs in sleep.
   — ALFRED TENNYSON.

LESSON 26.

Hard g as in get, marked ḡ.

1. Copy the following sentences carefully. 2. Write from dictation.

1. Youth is to all the *glad* season of life.
— Thomas Carlyle.

2. Where hast thou wandered, gentle *gale*, to find
The perfumes thou dost bring?
— William Cullen Bryant.

3. And see the waves so gently *glide*.— Robert Burns.

4.   Not a star
Shone, not a sound was heard; the very winds,
Danger's *grim* playmates, slept.
— Percy Bysshe Shelley.

5. The poorest *twig* on the elm-tree
Was ridged inch deep with pearl.
— James Russell Lowell.

6.   Those towers sublime,
That seemed above the *grasp* of Time.— Thomas Moore.

7. The brightness of their smile was *gone* from upland,
glade, and *glen*.— William Cullen Bryant.

8. Pride *goeth* forth on horseback *grand* and *gay*,
But cometh back on foot, and *begs* its way.
— Henry Wadsworth Longfellow.

9. His one ambition still to *get* and *get*,
He would arrest your very *ghost* for debt.
— James Russell Lowell.

ROBERT BURNS

1759 ⁕ 1796

LESSON 27.

Long u as in mute, marked ū.

1. Copy the following sentences carefully. 2. Write from dictation.

1. Sweet woodland *music* sinks and swells,
   The brooklet rings its tinkling bells.
   JOHN T. TROWBRIDGE.

2. And now it is an angel's song,
   That makes the heavens be *mute*.
   — SAMUEL TAYLOR COLERIDGE.

3. In sweet *music* is such art,
   Killing care and grief of heart
   Fall asleep. — WILLIAM SHAKESPEARE.

4. Come, pensive Nun, devout and *pure*,
   Sober, steadfast, and *demure*. — JOHN MILTON.

5. How small, of all that *human* hearts *endure*,
   That part which laws or kings can cause or *cure*.
   — OLIVER GOLDSMITH.

6. The wind, the wandering wind
   Of the golden summer eves —
   Whence is the thrilling magic
   Of its *tunes* amongst the leaves? — FELICIA D. HEMANS.

7. Life, like every other blessing,
   Derives its value from its *use* alone. — SAMUEL JOHNSON.

8. In the heaven that clear *obscure*,
   So softly dark, and darkly *pure*.
   — GEORGE GORDON, LORD BYRON.

LESSON 28.

Short u as in tub, marked ŭ.

1. Copy the following sentences carefully.   2. Write from dictation.

1. He lived one year in our orchard,
   From spring till fall, you see,
   And *swung* and *swung*, and *sung* and *sung*,
   In the top of the highest tree. — ALICE CARY.

2. Being all fashioned of the self-same *dust*,
   Let *us* be merciful as well as *just*.
   — HENRY WADSWORTH LONGFELLOW.

3.   There the *thrushes*
   Sing till the latest *sunlight flushes*
   In the west. — CHRISTINA G. ROSSETTI.

4.   Sing, Robin, sing!
   All among the reeds and *rushes*,
   Where the brook its music *hushes*. — SARAH F. DAVIS.

5. Yet Love will dream and Faith will *trust*
   (Since He who knows our need is *just*)
   That somehow, somewhere, meet we *must*.
   — JOHN GREENLEAF WHITTIER.

6. Avoid extremes; and *shun* the fault of *such*,
   Who still are pleased too little or too *much*.
   — ALEXANDER POPE.

7. And there never was water half so sweet
   As the draught that filled my *cup*,
   Drawn *up* to the curb by the rude old sweep
   That my father's hand set *up*. — PHŒBE CARY.

LESSON 29.
Review.

1. Copy the following sentences. Underscore all the words containing ŭ, or ū. 2. Write from dictation.

1. Its sunlit mountain tops are bathed
   In heaven's own blue. — JAMES A. GARFIELD.

2. Before green apples blush,
   Before green nuts embrown,
   Why, one day in the country
   Is worth a month in town. — CHRISTINA G. ROSSETTI.

3. I must go, I must run,
   Swifter than the fiery sun.
   — FRANCIS BEAUMONT AND JOHN FLETCHER.

4. Oh, how cruelly sweet are the echoes that start
   When Memory plays an old tune on the heart!
   — ELIZA COOK.

5. The faint fresh flame of the young year flushes,
   From leaf to flower and flower to fruit.
   — ALGERNON CHARLES SWINBURNE.

6. Music that gentlier on the spirit lies
   Than tir'd eyelids upon tir'd eyes. — ALFRED TENNYSON.

7. Only the actions of the just
   Smell sweet and blossom in the dust. — JAMES SHIRLEY.

8. Let us have faith that Right makes Might, and in that faith let us to the end dare to do our duty as we understand it. — ABRAHAM LINCOLN.

LESSON 30.

Sound of s as in has, marked ṣ = z.

1. Copy the following sentences carefully. 2. Write from dictation.

1. Are thy thoughts wandering to *elves* and *fays*,
   And spirits that dwell where the water *plays?*
   — Felicia D. Hemans.

2. He spoke of the grass and *flowers* and *trees*,
   Of the singing *birds* and humming *bees.*
   — John Greenleaf Whittier.

3.   Be *wise* with speed;
   A fool at forty *is* a fool indeed. — Edward Young.

4. Till painting gay the eastern *skies*,
   The glorious sun began to *rise.* — Robert Burns.

5. Sweet *was* the sound, when oft at *evening's close*,
   Up yonder hill the village murmur *rose.*
   — Oliver Goldsmith.

6. But why the wave *rises* and *kisses* the *rose*,
   And why the *rose* stoops for *those kisses* — who
   knows? — Edmund Waller.

7. The blackbird in the summer *trees*,
   The lark upon the hill,
   Let loose their *carols* when they *please*,
   Are quiet when they will. — William Wordsworth.

8. The *rose has* but a *summer's* reign,
   The *daisy* never *dies.* — James Montgomery.

LESSON 31.

1. Copy carefully.   2. Write from dictation, or from memory.

ROSES.

It is summer, says a fairy,
Bring me tissue light and airy;
Bring me colors of the rarest,
Search the rainbow for the fairest
Seashell pink, and sunny yellow,
Kingly crimson, deep and mellow;
Faint red in Aurora beaming,
And the white in pure pearl gleaming.

Bring me diamonds from the spaces
Where the air the earth embraces;
Bring me gold dust by divining
Where the humming-bird is mining;
Bring me sweets as rich as may be
From the kisses of a baby;
With an art no fay discloses
I am going to make some roses. — Anon.

I love it, I love it, the laugh of a child
Now rippling and gentle, now merry and wild;
Ringing out on the air with its innocent gush,
Like the trill of a bird at the twilight's soft hush;
Floating off on the breeze, like the tones of a bell,
Or the music that dwells in the heart of a shell;
Oh! the laugh of a child, so wild and so free,
Is the merriest sound in the world for me. — Anon.

LESSON 32.

Some words pronounced alike.

1. Copy carefully.   2. Write from dictation.   3. Use the italicized words in sentences of your own.

1. Heaven's *gate* is shut to him who comes alone.
   — JOHN GREENLEAF WHITTIER.

2. His form was bent, and his *gait* was slow,
   His long thin hair was white as snow.
   — GEORGE ARNOLD.

3. Green pastures she views in the midst of the dale,
   Down which she so often has tripped with her *pail*.
   WILLIAM WORDSWORTH.

4. Flowery May, who from her green lap throws
   The yellow cowslip, and the *pale* primrose.
   — JOHN MILTON.

5. Where village statesmen talked with looks profound,
   And news much older than their *ale* went round.
   — OLIVER GOLDSMITH.

6. I grew a *pale* and slender boy.
   I began to *ail* and mope.
   EDWARD BULWER, EARL LYTTON.

7. What *ails* thee, my poor child?
   — PERCY BYSSHE SHELLEY.

8. Many a *tale* of former day
   Shall wing the laughing hours away.
   — GEORGE GORDON, LORD BYRON.

9. Like Æsop's fox, when he had lost his *tail*, would have all his fellow-foxes cut off theirs.
   — ROBERT BURTON.

LESSON 33.

Broad a as in all, marked ą.

1. Copy the following sentences carefully. 2. Write from dictation.

1. He prayeth best who loveth best
   All things, both great and *small;*
   For the dear God who loveth us,
   He made and loveth *all*.—SAMUEL TAYLOR COLERIDGE.

2. Life and joy and health appear,
   Sweet Morning! at thy *call*.—FELICIA D. HEMANS.

3. In the leafy trees so broad and *tall*,
   Like a green and beautiful palace *hall*.—MARY HOWITT.

4. Yet oft a sigh prevails, and sorrows *fall*,
   To see the hoard of human bliss so *small*.
   —OLIVER GOLDSMITH.

5. The fish swam by the castle *wall*,
   And they seem'd joyous each and *all*.
   —GEORGE GORDON, LORD BYRON.

6. Laughed the brook for my delight
   Through the day and through the night,
   Whispering at the garden *wall*,
   Talked with me from *fall* to *fall*.
   —JOHN GREENLEAF WHITTIER.

7. He gathered the ripe nuts in the *fall*,
   And berries that grew by fence and *wall*
   So high she could not reach them *all*.—PHŒBE CARY.

8. We'll gently *walk* and sweetly *talk*.—ROBERT BURNS.

LESSON 34.

Flowers.

1. Copy carefully. 2. Write from dictation, or from memory.

1. Said young Dandelion
   With a sweet air,
   I have my eye on
   Miss Daisy fair. — DINAH MARIA MULOCK.

2. I lie amid the goldenrod,
   I love to see it lean and nod. — MARY CLEMMER.

3. Oh! roses and lilies are fair to see;
   But the wild bluebell is the flower for me.
   — LOUISA A. MEREDITH.

4. A violet by a mossy stone
   Half hidden from the eye!
   Fair as a star, when only one
   Is shining in the sky. — WILLIAM WORDSWORTH.

5. Of all the bonny buds that blow
   In bright or cloudy weather,
   Of all the flowers that come and go
   The whole twelve moons together,
   The little purple pansy brings
   Thoughts of the sweetest, saddest things.
   — MARY E. BRADLEY.

6. When on the breath of Autumn's breeze,
   From pastures dry and brown,
   Goes floating, like an idle thought,
   The fair, white thistle-down. — MARY HOWITT.

LESSON 35.

Broad o as in gone, marked ó.

This sound is between *o* in *not*, and *a* in *all*.

1. Copy the following sentences carefully. 2. Write from dictation.

1. The woods were fill'd so full of *song*,
   There seem'd no room for sense of *wrong*.
   — ALFRED TENNYSON.

2. In dark and silence hidden *long*,
   The brook repeats its summer *song*.
   — JOHN GREENLEAF WHITTIER.

3. The river forever glides singing *along*,
   The rose on the bank bends down to its *song*.
   — EDMUND WALLER.

4. And I envy thy stream, as it glides *along*
   Through its beautiful banks in a trance of *song*.
   WILLIAM CULLEN BRYANT.

5. What's *gone* and what's past help should be past grief. — WILLIAM SHAKESPEARE.

6. Our life contains a thousand springs,
   And dies if one be *gone*,
   Strange! that a harp of a thousand strings
   Should keep in tune so *long*. — ISAAC WATTS.

7. *Soft* as the memory of buried love,
   Pure as the prayer which childhood wafts above.
   — GEORGE GORDON, LORD BYRON.

8. A bell was tolled in that far-*off* town,
   For one who had passed from *cross* to crown.
   — HENRY WADSWORTH LONGFELLOW.

LESSON 36.

Some words pronounced alike.

1. Copy carefully. 2. Write from dictation. 3. Use the italicized words in sentences of your own.

1. As *dear* to me as are the ruddy drops
   That visit my sad heart.— WILLIAM SHAKESPEARE.

2. Where the *deer's* swift leap
   Startles the wild bee from the foxglove bell.
   — JOHN KEATS.

3. Oh, God! that bread should be so *dear*,
   And flesh and blood so cheap.— THOMAS HOOD.

4. Fair hands the broken grain shall sift,
   And *knead* its meal of gold.— JOHN GREENLEAF WHITTIER.

5. He that is thy friend indeed,
   He will help thee in thy *need*.— WILLIAM SHAKESPEARE.

6. They are slaves who fear to speak
   For the fallen and the *weak*.— JAMES RUSSELL LOWELL.

7. What, keep a *week* away? seven days and nights?
   Eight score and eight hours?— WILLIAM SHAKESPEARE.

8. If any man hath ears to *hear*, let him *hear*.
   And he said unto them, Take heed what ye *hear*.
   — BIBLE.

9. Spring and Autumn *here*
   Danc'd hand in hand.— JOHN MILTON.

10. Hark! I *hear* music on the zephyr's wing.
    — PERCY BYSSHE SHELLEY.

LESSON 37.

Italian a as in far, marked ä.

1. Copy the following sentences carefully. 2. Write from dictation.

1. A rainbow's *arch* stood on the sea.
 — PERCY BYSSHE SHELLEY.

2. No tree in all the grove but has its *charm*.
 — WILLIAM COWPER.

3. The birch trees wept in fragrant *balm*,
 The aspens slept beneath the *calm*. — SIR WALTER SCOTT.

4. The *stars* come forth to listen
 To the music of the sea.
 — HENRY WADSWORTH LONGFELLOW.

5.   *Hark!* on the winds
 The bell's deep tones are swelling.
 — GEORGE D. PRENTICE.

6. How often have I paused on every *charm*,
 The sheltered cot, the cultivated *farm*.
 — OLIVER GOLDSMITH.

7. *Dark* and more *dark* the shades of evening fell.
 WILLIAM WORDSWORTH.

8. See where, upon the horizon's brim,
 Lies the still cloud in gloomy *bars;*
 The waning moon, all pale and dim,
 Goes up amid the eternal *stars*.
 — WILLIAM CULLEN BRYANT.

9. A tempest howling through the *dark*,
 A crash as of some shipwrecked *bark*.
 — HENRY WADSWORTH LONGFELLOW.

LESSON 38.

Birds.

1. Copy carefully.   2. Write from dictation, or from memory.

1. A goldfinch there I saw, with gaudy pride
   Of painted plumes, that hopped from side to side.
   — JOHN DRYDEN.

2. The birds of morning trim their bustling wings,
   And listen fondly — while the blackbird sings.
   — FREDERICK TENNYSON.

3. Among the dwellings framed by birds
   In field or forest with nice care,
   Is none that with the little wren's
   In snugness may compare. — WILLIAM WORDSWORTH.

4. O Bluebird, up in the maple tree,
   Shaking your throat with such bursts of glee,
   How did you happen to be so blue?
   Did you steal a bit of the sky for your crest,
   And fasten blue violets into your breast?
   Tell me, I pray you, tell me true! — SAMUEL SWETT.

5. The merry lark he soars on high,
   No worldly thought o'ertakes him.
   He sings aloud to the clear blue sky,
   And the daylight that awakes him.
   — HARTLEY COLERIDGE.

6. Linnet and meadowlark, and all the throng
   That dwell in nests, and have the gift of song.
   — HENRY WADSWORTH LONGFELLOW.

LESSON 39.

Variant a as in ask, marked ä.

This sound is between *a* in *hat,* and *a* in *far.*
1. Copy the following sentences carefully. 2. Write from dictation.

1. A fool must now and then be right by *chance.*
 — WILLIAM COWPER.

2. Feast, and your halls will be crowded;
 Fast, and the world goes by. — ELLA WHEELER WILCOX.

3. The windows rattled with the *blast,*
 The oak trees shouted as it *passed.*
 — HENRY WADSWORTH LONGFELLOW.

4. When the shore is won at *last,*
 Who will count the billows *past?* — JOHN KEBLE.

5. To watch the colors that flit and *pass*
 With insect wings, through the wavy *grass.*
 — FELICIA D. HEMANS.

6. 'Tis not on youth's smooth cheek the blush alone, which fades so *fast,*
 But the tender bloom of heart is gone ere youth itself be *past.* — GEORGE GORDON, LORD BYRON.

7. There is not wind enough to twirl
 The one red leaf, the *last* of its clan,
 That *dances* as often as *dance* it can,
 Hanging so light and hanging so high,
 On the topmost twig that looks up to the sky.
 — SAMUEL TAYLOR COLERIDGE.

LESSON 40.

Some words pronounced alike.

1. Copy carefully. 2. Write from dictation. 3. Use the italicized words in sentences of your own.

1. The shepherds on the lawn,
   Or ere the point of dawn,
   Sat simply chatting in a rustic *row*. — JOHN MILTON.

2. Chasing the wild deer, and following the *roe* —
   My heart's in the Highlands wherever I go.
   ROBERT BURNS.

3. *Row*, brothers, *row*, the stream runs fast,
   The rapids are near, and the daylight's past!
   THOMAS MOORE.

4. O life! thou art a galling load,
   Along a rough, a weary *road!* — ROBERT BURNS.

5. Swift summer into the autumn flowed,
   And frost in the mist of the morning *rode*.
   — PERCY BYSSHE SHELLEY.

6.   The sailors *rowed*
   In awe. — PERCY BYSSHE SHELLEY.

7. Each boatman, bending to his *oar*,
   With measured sweep the burden bore.
   — SIR WALTER SCOTT.

8. Th' allotted hour of daily sport is *o'er*,
   And Learning beckons from her temple's door.
   GEORGE GORDON, LORD BYRON.

9. Thy form and mind, sweet maid, can I forget?
   In richest *ore* the brightest jewel set! — ROBERT BURNS.

LESSON 41.

Narrow **a** as in **care**, marked â. âi = â.

1. Copy the following sentences carefully. 2. Write from dictation.

1. Graceful and tall as a lily *fair*,
    The peach lent the bloom to her blushes *rare*,
    And the thrush the brown of her rippling *hair*.
    — PHŒBE CARY.

2. The sweetest flowers are ever frail and *rare*.
    — PERCY BYSSHE SHELLEY.

3. Not what we give, but what we *share*, —
    For the gift without the giver is *bare*.
    JAMES RUSSELL LOWELL.

4. The voice so sweet, the word so *fair*,
    As some soft chime had stroked the *air*. — BEN JONSON.

5.   O holy Night!
    Thou layest thy finger on the lips of *Care*.
    — HENRY WADSWORTH LONGFELLOW.

6. Time was when I was free as *air*,
    The thistle's downy seed my *fare*,
    My drink the morning dew. — WILLIAM COWPER.

7. But me, not destined such delights to *share*,
    My prime of life in wandering spent and *care*.
    — OLIVER GOLDSMITH.

8. I love it, I love it; and who shall *dare*
    To chide me for loving the old arm*chair*?
    — ELIZA COOK.

LESSON 42.

ĕa = e short, marked ĕ.

1. Copy the following sentences carefully. 2. Write from dictation.

1. How wonderful is *Death*,
   Death and his brother sleep! — Percy Bysshe Shelley.

2. Boughs where the thrush, with crimson *breast*,
   Shall haunt, and sing, and hide her nest.
   William Cullen Bryant.

3. The low of cattle and song of birds,
   And *health* and quiet and loving words.
   — John Greenleaf Whittier.

4.   On the mountain's *head*,
   Moonlight and snow their mingling luster *spread*.
   Felicia D. Hemans.

5. Closed are the pink and the poppy red,
   And the lily near them hangs her *head*. — Phœbe Cary.

6.   A simple child,
   That lightly draws its *breath*,
   And feels its life in every limb,
   What should it know of *death?* — William Wordsworth.

7. At every *breath* were balmy odors shed,
   Which still grew sweeter as they wider *spread*.
   — Alexander Pope.

8. I count my *health* my greatest *wealth*. — Robert Burns.

9. Ah, but a man's reach should exceed his grasp,
   Or what's a *heaven* for? — Robert Browning.

WILLIAM WORDSWORTH

1770 ⚜ 1850

LESSON 43.

Some words pronounced alike.

1. Copy carefully.   2. Write from dictation.   3. Use the italicized words in sentences of your own.

1.   And often too
A little cloud would move across the *blue*.
— JOHN KEATS.

2. Oh, *blue* were violets in our youth and *blue* were April skies,
And *blue* the early song bird's wings, but *bluer* were the eyes
That in the land of long ago looked through the window pane
And saw the pansies shut their lids against the slanting rain. — ROBERT MCINTYRE.

3. The light wind *blew* from the gates of the sun,
And waves of shadow went over the wheat.
— ALFRED TENNYSON.

4. Truly, sir, *all* that I live by is the *awl*.
WILLIAM SHAKESPEARE.

5. Wisdom and worth were *all* he had,
But these were *all* to me. — OLIVER GOLDSMITH.

6. *To* know, *to* esteem, *to* love, — and then *to* part,
Makes up life's tale *to* many a feeling heart.
SAMUEL TAYLOR COLERIDGE.

7. The visions of my youth are past,
Too bright, *too* beautiful *to* last.
— WILLIAM CULLEN BRYANT.

8. 'Tis not a year or *two* shows us a man.
— WILLIAM SHAKESPEARE.

LESSON 44.

Long **oo** as in **moon**, marked o͞o.

1. Copy the following sentences carefully. 2. Write from dictation.

1. Damask roses in full *bloom*,
   Making a garden of the *room*.
   HENRY WADSWORTH LONGFELLOW.

2. Who loves not more the night of June
   Than dull December's *gloomy noon?*
   — SIR WALTER SCOTT.

3. The *moon* is at her full, and, riding high,
   Floods the calm fields with light.
   — WILLIAM CULLEN BRYANT.

4. Thus done the tales, to bed they creep,
   By whispering winds *soon* lull'd asleep. — JOHN MILTON.

5. 'Tis an old maxim in the *schools*,
   That flattery is the *food* of *fools.* — JONATHAN SWIFT.

6. Many a word, at random spoken,
   May *soothe* or wound a heart that's broken.
   SIR WALTER SCOTT.

7. The scented birch and hawthorn white
   Across the *pool* their arms unite. — ROBERT BURNS.

8. Clear and *cool*, clear and *cool*,
   By laughing shallow, and dreaming *pool*.
   CHARLES KINGSLEY.

9. His heart was as great as the world, but there was no *room* in it to hold the memory of a wrong.
   — RALPH WALDO EMERSON.

LESSON 45.

Short oo as in foot, marked ŏŏ.

1. Copy the following sentences carefully. 2. Write from dictation.

1. In every breeze what aspens *shook*,
   What alders shaded every *brook!* — Sir Walter Scott.

2. To thee my fancy *took* its wing. — Robert Burns.

3. The purple asters bloom in crowds
   In every shady *nook*. — Dora R. Goodale.

4. Sighing every minute and groaning every hour would detect the lazy *foot* of Time as well as a clock.
   — William Shakespeare.

5. Fresh grasses fringe the meadow *brooks*,
   And mildly from its sunny *nooks*
   The blue eye of the violet *looks*.
   — John Greenleaf Whittier.

6. And schoolgirls, gay with aster-flowers, beside the meadow *brooks*,
   Mingled the glow of autumn with the sunshine of sweet *looks*. — John Greenleaf Whittier.

7. I thought of a mound in sweet Auburn,
   Where a little headstone *stood;*
   How the flakes were folding it gently,
   As did robins the babes in the *wood*.
   — James Russell Lowell.

LESSON 46.

Birds.

1. Copy carefully. 2. Write from dictation, or from memory.

1. O Cuckoo! shall I call thee Bird,
   Or but a wandering Voice?—WILLIAM WORDSWORTH.

2. Is it for thee the linnet pours his throat?
   Loves of his own, and raptures swell the note.
   —ALEXANDER POPE.

3. That's the wise thrush; he sings each song twice over,
   Lest you should think he never could recapture
   The first fine careless rapture!—ROBERT BROWNING.

4.   The nightingale
   Was pausing in her heaven-taught tale!
   —PERCY BYSSHE SHELLEY.

5. On the cross beam under the Old South bell,
   The nest of a pigeon is builded well.
   —NATHANIEL P. WILLIS.

6. The robin warbled forth his full clear note
   For hours, and wearied not.—WILLIAM CULLEN BRYANT.

7. The swallow twitters about the eaves;
   Blithely she sings, and sweet, and clear;
   Around her climb the woodbine leaves
   In a golden atmosphere.—CELIA THAXTER.

8. Hark! Hark! the lark at heaven's gate sings.
   —WILLIAM SHAKESPEARE.

LESSON 47.

1. Copy carefully.   2. Write from dictation, or from memory.

But when the patient stars look down
  On all their light discovers,
The traitor's smile, the murderer's frown,
  The lips of lying lovers,

They try to shut their saddening eyes,
  And in the vain endeavor
We see them twinkling in the skies,
  And so they wink forever.
OLIVER WENDELL HOLMES.

Earth, with her thousand voices, praises God.
— SAMUEL TAYLOR COLERIDGE.

I shall speak of trees as we see them, love them, adore them in the fields, where they are alive, holding their green sunshades over our heads, talking to us with their hundred thousand whispering tongues.
— OLIVER WENDELL HOLMES.

Sunday afternoon the birds were sweetly mad, and the lovely rage of song drove them hither and thither, and swelled their breasts amain. It was nothing less than a tornado of fine music. I kept saying, "Yes, yes, yes, I know, dear little maniacs! I know there never was such an air, such a day, such a sky, such a God! I know it,—I know it!" But they would not be pacified. Their throats must have been made of fine gold, or they would have been rent by such rapture quakes.

— MRS. NATHANIEL HAWTHORNE (in a letter to her mother).

LESSON 48.

Some words pronounced alike.

1. Copy carefully. 2. Write from dictation. 3. Use the italicized words in sentences of your own.

1. With kind words and kinder looks, he *bade* me go my way.—JOHN GREENLEAF WHITTIER.

2. *Bad* men excuse their faults, good men will leave them.—BEN JONSON.

3. Then as to greet the sunbeam's birth,
Rises the choral *hymn* of earth.—FELICIA D. HEMANS.

4. He was a man, take *him* for all in all,
I shall not look upon his like again.
—WILLIAM SHAKESPEARE.

5. He who knows most, grieves most for wasted *time*.
—DANTE.

6.   And desert caves
With wild *thyme* and the gadding vine o'ergrown.
JOHN MILTON.

7. Tell not as *new* what everybody knows,
And *new* or old, still hasten to a close.
—WILLIAM COWPER.

8. And still they gazed, and still the wonder grew,
That one small head could carry all he *knew*.
—OLIVER GOLDSMITH.

9. It *ate* the food it ne'er had eat,
And round and round it flew.
—SAMUEL TAYLOR COLERIDGE.

10. I have studied *eight* or nine wise words to speak to you.—WILLIAM SHAKESPEARE.

LESSON 49.

Sound of oi as in oil, unmarked.

1. Copy the following sentences carefully. 2. Write from dictation.

1. Till the Alps replied to that *voice* of war
   With a thousand of their own. — FELICIA D. HEMANS.

2.   In every *soil*
   Those that think must govern those that *toil*.
                                 OLIVER GOLDSMITH.

3. We *join* ourselves to no party that does not carry the flag and keep step to the music of the union.
                                 — RUFUS CHOATE.

4. The church spires *point* as with silent finger to the sky and stars. — SAMUEL TAYLOR COLERIDGE.

5. In morning's smile its eddies *coil*,
   Its billows sparkle, toss, and *boil*.
                                 — PERCY BYSSHE SHELLEY.

6.   We gather flowery *spoils*
   From land and water. — WILLIAM WORDSWORTH.

7. Yonder bank hath *choice* of sun and shade.
                                 — JOHN MILTON.

8. Where the sweet winds did gently kiss the trees
   And they did make no *noise*. — WILLIAM SHAKESPEARE.

9. Where with black cliffs the torrents *toil*
   He watch'd the wheeling eddies *boil*.
                                 SIR WALTER SCOTT.

LESSON 50.

Sound of **ou** as in **out**, unmarked.

1. Copy the following sentences carefully. 2. Write from dictation.

1. It's hardly in a body's power
   To keep at times from being *sour.* — ROBERT BURNS.

2.   In flowery June,
   When brooks send up a cheerful tune,
   And groves a joyous *sound.* — WILLIAM CULLEN BRYANT.

3. And waves on the *outer* rocks afoam
   Shout to its waters, "Welcome home!"
                                 — JOHN GREENLEAF WHITTIER.

4. In the elms, — a noisy crowd!
   All the birds are singing *loud.*— MARY HOWITT.

5. The *proud* are always most provoked by pride.
                                 WILLIAM COWPER.

6. Where weeping birch and willow *round,*
   With their long fibers swept the *ground.*
                                 — SIR WALTER SCOTT.

7. It was a voice so mellow, so bright and warm and
      round,
   As if a beam of sunshine had been melted into *sound.*
                                 HJALMAR H. BOYESEN.

8. Words are like leaves; and where they most *abound,*
   Much fruit of sense beneath is rarely *found.*
                                 — ALEXANDER POPE.

LESSON 51.

Sound of ow as in how, unmarked.

1. Copy the following sentences carefully. 2. Write from dictation.

1. Often in thought I go up and *down*
   The pleasant streets of the dear old *town*.
   — Henry Wadsworth Longfellow.

2. The sun had on a *crown*
   Wrought of gilded *thistle-down*,
   And a scarf of velvet vapor
   And a raveled rainbow *gown*. — James Whitcomb Riley.

3. *Crowds* of bees are busy with clover,
   Crowds of grasshoppers skip at my feet.
   — Jean Ingelow.

4. And muffled *growls*, like the *growl* of a beast,
   Ran along the sky from west to east.
   — John Greenleaf Whittier.

5. O'er yon bare knoll the pointed cedar shadows
   Drowse on the crisp gray moss. — James Russell Lowell.

6. All nature mourns, the skies relent in *showers*,
   Hush'd are the birds, and closed the drooping *flowers*.
   — Alexander Pope.

7. What though the sun, with ardent *frown*,
   Had slightly tinged her cheek with *brown*.
   — Sir Walter Scott.

8. The arts of building from the bee receive,
   Learn of the mole to *plow*, the worm to weave.
   — Alexander Pope.

LESSON 52.

Obscure e as in her, marked ẽ.

1. Copy the following sentences carefully. 2. Write from dictation.

1. The voice of cool *waters* 'midst *feathery fern*,
   Shedding sweet sounds.— Felicia D. Hemans.

2. And the *verse* of that dear old song,
   It *flutters* and murmurs still.
   — Henry Wadsworth Longfellow.

3. On the tawny sands and shelves
   Trip the *pert* fairies and *dapper* elves.— John Milton.

4. No noise was *heard* but of the hasty brook.
   William Cowper.

5. The lowing *herd* winds slowly o'er the lea.
   Thomas Gray.

6. And each flower and *herb* on *Earth's* dark breast
   Rose from the dreams of its wintry rest.
   — Percy Bysshe Shelley.

7. A poet, too, was there, whose *verse*
   Was *tender*, musical, and *terse*.
   — Henry Wadsworth Longfellow.

8. No price is set on the lavish *summer;*
   June may be had by the poorest *comer*.
   — James Russell Lowell.

9. They only knew
   That the *earth* was bright and the sky was blue.
   — Anon.

10. And man may *err*, but no one but a fool will persevere in error.— Cicero.

LESSON 53.

Some words pronounced alike.

1. Copy carefully. 2. Write from dictation. 3. Use the italicized words in sentences of your own.

1. There will little learning *die* then, that day thou art hanged.—WILLIAM SHAKESPEARE.

2. Come thou with me to the vineyards nigh,
   And we'll pluck the grapes of the richest *dye*.
   —FELICIA D. HEMANS.

3. If any one attempts to *haul* down the American flag, shoot him on the spot.—JOHN A. DIX.

4. Be merry all, be merry all,
   With holly dress the festive *hall*.—WILLIAM R. SPENCER.

5. When youth and pleasure meet
   To chase the glowing hours with flying *feet*.
   —GEORGE GORDON, LORD BYRON.

6. In all the trade of war, no *feat*
   Is nobler than a brave retreat.—SAMUEL BUTLER.

7. Wild as the winter now tearing the forest,
   Till the last *leaf* of summer is flown.—ROBERT BURNS.

8. She, good soul, had as *lief* see a toad, a very toad, as see him.—WILLIAM SHAKESPEARE.

9. Let me see; is not the *leaf* turn'd down
   Where I left reading?—WILLIAM SHAKESPEARE.

LESSON 54.

Obscure i as in **sir**, marked ĭ.

1. Copy the following sentences carefully. 2. Write from dictation.

1.   A fresher gale
Begins to wave the wood, and *stir* the stream.
           —JAMES THOMSON.

2. I read in each tint of the skies and the earth
How distant my steps from the land of my *birth*.
          —FELICIA D. HEMANS.

3. The groves were God's *first* temples.
        —WILLIAM CULLEN BRYANT.

4. And mingled in its merry *whirl*
The grandam and the laughing *girl*.
        JOHN GREENLEAF WHITTIER.

5. By fairy hands their knell is rung,
By forms unseen their *dirge* is sung.—WILLIAM COLLINS.

6.   The clocks do toll,
And the *third* hour of drowsy morning name.
        — WILLIAM SHAKESPEARE.

7. He, who called with thought to *birth*
Yon tinted sky, this laughing earth. — WILLIAM COLLINS.

8. I heard the distant waters dash,
I saw the current *whirl* and flash.
       — HENRY WADSWORTH LONGFELLOW.

9.   Work and *mirth* and play
Unite their charms to cheer the hours away.
         —JOEL BARLOW.

LESSON 55.

Some words pronounced alike.

1. Copy carefully. 2. Write from dictation. 3. Use the italicized words in sentences of your own.

1. Bring flowers to the captive's lonely *cell!*
   They have tales of the joyous woods to tell.
   — FELICIA D. HEMANS.

2. I will buy with you, *sell* with you, talk with you, walk with you, but I will not eat with you, drink with you, nor pray with you.
   — WILLIAM SHAKESPEARE.

3. *One* flag, *one* land, *one* heart, *one* hand,
   One Nation evermore! — OLIVER WENDELL HOLMES.

4. Learning by study must be *won.* — JOHN GAY.

5. Beds of violets blue,
   And fresh-blown roses wash'd in *dew.* — JOHN MILTON.

6. We receive the *due* reward of our deeds. — BIBLE.

7. More is thy *due* than more than all can pay.
   — WILLIAM SHAKESPEARE.

8. He faded, and *so* calm and meek,
   So softly worn, *so* sweetly weak,
   So tearless, yet *so* tender.
   — GEORGE GORDON, LORD BYRON.

9. To plow and *sow,* to reap and mow. — ROBERT BURNS.

10. She can *sew.* — That's as much as to say, Can she *so?* — WILLIAM SHAKESPEARE.

LESSON 56.

Obscure u as in **fur**, marked ū.

1. Copy the following sentences carefully. 2. Write from dictation.

1. At every *turn* the maples *burn*,
   The quail is whistling free,
   The partridge whirs and the frosted *burrs*
   Are dropping for you and me. — EDMUND C. STEDMAN.

2. You may as well go about to *turn* the sun to ice with fanning in his face with a peacock's feather.
   — WILLIAM SHAKESPEARE.

3. Hope ever *urges* on, and tells us to-morrow will be better. — TIBULLUS.

4. Away its hurrying waters break,
   Faster and whiter dash and *curl*,
   Till down yon dark abyss they *hurl*.
   — SIR WALTER SCOTT.

5. How sweet from the green mossy brim to receive it,
   As, poised on the *curb*, it inclined to my lips!
   — SAMUEL WOODWORTH.

6. Sunk to a *curve* the daystar lessens still,
   Gives one bright glance, and drops behind the hill.
   WILLIAM WORDSWORTH.

7. The budding groves appeared as if in haste
   To *spur* the steps of June. — WILLIAM WORDSWORTH.

8. We were the first that ever *burst*
   Into that silent sea. — SAMUEL TAYLOR COLERIDGE.

LESSON 57.

Some words pronounced alike.

1. Copy carefully.   2. Write from dictation.   3. Use the italicized words in sentences of your own.

1. She's too low for a high *praise*, too brown for a fair *praise*, and too little for a great *praise*.
   —William Shakespeare.

2. The Saint, the Father, and the Husband *prays*.
   — Robert Burns.

3. The letter is too long *by* half a mile.
   — William Shakespeare.

4. I would not spend another such a night,
   Though 'twere to *buy* a world of happy days.
   — William Shakespeare.

5. Good-*by*, proud world! I'm going home.
   — Ralph Waldo Emerson.

6. To *hie* him home, at evening's close,
   To sweet repast and calm repose.— Thomas Gray.

7.   There, on *high*,
   Where mountain snows are mingling with the sky.
   Felicia D. Hemans.

8. A voice, whose tones are sweet and wild,
   Singing a song almost divine,
   And with a *tear* in every line.
   — Henry Wadsworth Longfellow.

9. The muskrat plied the mason's trade,
   And *tier* by *tier* his mudwalls laid.
   —John Greenleaf Whittier.

LESSON 58.

Birds.

1. Copy carefully. 2. Write from dictation, or from memory.

1. The whip-poor-will, her name her only song.
— CARLOS WILCOX.

2. And the humming bird that hung
Like a jewel up among
The tilted honeysuckle horns. — JAMES WHITCOMB RILEY.

3. Modest and shy as a nun is she,
One weak chirp is her only note;
Braggart and prince of braggarts is he,
Pouring boasts from his little throat:
Bobolink, bobolink. — WILLIAM CULLEN BRYANT.

4. And there my little doves did sit
With feathers softly brown,
And glittering eyes that showed their right
To general Nature's deep delight.
ELIZABETH BARRETT BROWNING.

5. The eagle rode the rising blast,
Methought he never flew so fast
As then to me he seem'd to fly,
And then new tears came in my eye.
— GEORGE GORDON, LORD BYRON.

6. It was the carol of a bird;
It ceased, and then it came again,
The sweetest song ear ever heard.
— GEORGE GORDON, LORD BYRON.

LESSON 59.

Obscure **o** as in **word** = **u** in **fur**, and nearly = **e** in **her**, and **i** in **sir**.

1. Copy carefully. 2. Write from dictation.

1. Of sunshine wilt thou think, and flower and song,
And breathe as in a *world* where nothing can go wrong.—WILLIAM WORDSWORTH.

2. Every one is as God made him, and ofttimes a great deal *worse*.—CERVANTES.

3.   Knowest thou when Fate
Thy measure takes, or when she'll say to thee,
"I find thee *worthy*; do this deed for me?"
        —JAMES RUSSELL LOWELL.

4.   *Labor*
Knocked with its hundred hands at the golden gates of the morning.—HENRY WADSWORTH LONGFELLOW.

5. We should try to succeed by merit, not by *favor*.
        —PLAUTUS.

6. An honest man's the noblest *work* of God.
        —ALEXANDER POPE.

7. No clouds are in the morning sky,
The *vapors* hug the stream,
Who says that life and love can die
In all this northern gleam?—EDMUND C. STEDMAN.

8. *Worth* makes the man, and want of it the fellow.
        —ALEXANDER POPE.

9. I'll be a poet and paint with *words*
Talking children and chirping birds.—ALICE CARY.

LESSON 60.

Some words pronounced alike.

1. Copy carefully. 2. Write from dictation. 3. Use the italicized words in sentences of your own.

1. So *be* it, for it cannot *be* but so.
— WILLIAM SHAKESPEARE.

2. The *bee* that through the sunny hour
    Sips nectar in the op'ning flower. — ROBERT BURNS.

3. Now were instituted "quilting bees" and "husking bees." — WASHINGTON IRVING.

4. A fretful temper will divide
    The closest *knot* that may be tied. — WILLIAM COWPER.

5. O time! thou must untangle this, *not* I;
    It is too hard a *knot* for me to untie!
— WILLIAM SHAKESPEARE.

6. For *in* the *inn* was left no better room.
JOHN MILTON.

7. And ere the stars were visible, had reached
    A village *inn*, — our evening resting-place.
— WILLIAM WORDSWORTH.

8. But hark! a *rap* comes gently to the door.
— ROBERT BURNS.

9. Or *wrap* himself in Hamlet's inky cloak.
— WILLIAM COWPER.

10. Thou flea, thou *nit*, thou winter cricket thou!
WILLIAM SHAKESPEARE.

11. Still closer *knit* in friendship's ties
    Each passing year! — ROBERT BURNS.

LESSON 61.

Sound of u as in rude, marked ų.

1. Copy the following sentences carefully. 2. Write from dictation.

1. There is a temple in *ruin* stands,
   Fashioned by long-forgotten hands.
   GEORGE GORDON, LORD BYRON

2. Whose rills o'er *ruby* beds and topaz flow,
   Catching the gem's bright color, as they go.
   THOMAS MOORE.

3. In fact, there is nothing that keeps its youth,
   So far as I know, but a tree and *truth*.
   — OLIVER WENDELL HOLMES.

4.   Each *rude* recess,
   Where the deep echo slept in loneliness.
   FELICIA D. HEMANS.

5. One of the best *rules* of conversation is, never to say a thing which any of the company can reasonably wish unsaid. — JONATHAN SWIFT.

6. Morning rises into noon,
   May glides onward into *June*.
   — SAMUEL TAYLOR COLERIDGE.

7. The flying *rumors* gather'd as they roll'd,
   Scarce any tale was sooner heard than told.
   — ALEXANDER POPE.

8. 'Tis as easy now for the heart to be *true*
   As for grass to be green or skies to be *blue*.
   — JAMES RUSSELL LOWELL.

LESSON 62.

Signs used for a as in hate.

$\overset{1}{\text{ai}}, \overset{2}{\text{ay}}, \overset{3}{\text{ei}}, \overset{4}{\text{ey}}, \overset{5}{\text{ea}}, \overset{6}{\text{au}} = \bar{\text{a}}.$

1. Copy the following sentences. 2. Write from dictation.

1. When at *break*[5] of *day*,[2]
    On the tall peaks the glistening sunbeams *play*.[2]
    — WILLIAM WORDSWORTH.

2. As she fled fast thro' sun and shade,
    The happy winds upon her *play'd*,[2]
    Blowing the ringlet from the *braid*.[1]
    — ALFRED TENNYSON.

3. The first *faint*[1] streaks of light purpling the East,
    which the lark springs up to greet.
    — DANIEL WEBSTER.

4. What millions died that Cæsar might be *great!*[5]
    — THOMAS CAMPBELL.

5. The reason why the seven stars are no more than seven is a pretty reason. — Because *they*[4] are not *eight?*[3] — WILLIAM SHAKESPEARE.

6. Had seen the mice by moonlight *play*,[2]
    And why should I feel less than *they?*[4]
    — GEORGE GORDON, LORD BYRON.

7. Lands he could measure, terms and tides presage,
    And e'en the story ran that he could *gauge*.[6]
    — OLIVER GOLDSMITH.

8. Striving not to be rich or *great*,[5]
    Never questioning fortune or fate,
    Contented slowly to earn, and *wait*.[1] — PHŒBE CARY.

SIR WALTER SCOTT

1 7 7 1   ⁕   1 8 3 2

LESSON 63.

Signs used for a as in far.

$\overset{1}{\text{äu}}$, $\overset{2}{\text{eä}}$, $\overset{3}{\text{uä}}$ = ä.

1. Copy the following sentences.   2. Write from dictation.

1. Far from the cheerful *haunt*[1] of men and herds.
— JOHN MILTON.
2. Evening's peace falls gently on the *heart*.[2]
— JAMES A. GARFIELD.
3. God and his angels *guard*[3] your sacred throne!
— WILLIAM SHAKESPEARE.

Some words pronounced alike.

1. I wish no living thing to suffer *pain*.
— PERCY BYSSHE SHELLEY.
2. As down the *pane* the rival raindrops chase,
Curious he'll watch to see which wins the race.
— CHARLES SPRAGUE.
3. The earth had not a *hole* to hide this deed.
— WILLIAM SHAKESPEARE.
4.   Wildly here without control,
Nature reigns and rules the *whole*. — ROBERT BURNS.

5. You are *hale*, Father William, — a hearty old man:
Now tell me the reason, I pray. — ROBERT SOUTHEY.

6. *Hail*, Columbia! happy land!
Hail, ye heroes! heaven-born band!
— JOSEPH HOPKINSON.
7. Where falls not *hail*, or rain, or any snow,
Nor ever wind blows loudly. — ALFRED TENNYSON.

LESSON 64.

Signs used for a as in all.

$\overset{1}{\text{aw}}, \overset{2}{\text{au}}, \overset{3}{\text{ôu}}, \overset{4}{\text{ô}}, \overset{5}{\text{eô}}, \overset{6}{\text{oa}} = \text{a}.$

1. Copy the following sentences. 2. Write from dictation.

1. But I struck one *chord*[4] of music,
   Like the sound of a great Amen.
   — ADELAIDE A. PROCTER.

2. Now danced the lights on *lawn*[1] and lea.
   — ALFRED TENNYSON.

3. Each girl, when pleased with what is *taught*,[2]
   Will have the teacher in her *thought*.[3]
   — JONATHAN SWIFT.

4. To be without evil *thoughts*[3] is God's best gift.
   — ÆSCHYLUS.

5. He trudg'd along unknowing what he *sought*,[3]
   And whistled as he went, for want of *thought*.[3]
   — JOHN DRYDEN.

6. But bless the scroll which fairer words *adorn*,[4]
   Traced by the rosy finger of the *morn*.[4]
   — GEORGE GORDON, LORD BYRON.

7. Almost upon the western wave,
   Rested the *broad*[6] bright sun.
   — SAMUEL TAYLOR COLERIDGE.

8. Cry 'God for Harry, England and Saint *George!*[5]'
   WILLIAM SHAKESPEARE.

9. Tints of the sun whose bright farewell is *fraught*[2]
   With all that art hath dreamt, but never *caught*.[2]
   — FELICIA D. HEMANS.

LESSON 65.

Signs used for a as in care.

ái[1], eâ[2], ĕi[3], ê[4] = a.

1. Copy the following sentences. 2. Write from dictation.

1. But what can give pleasure, or what can seem *fair*,[1]
When the lingering moments are numbered with care?—ROBERT BURNS.

2. *Airs*[1] that on *their*[3] errands sped
And wild birds gossiping overhead.
— HENRY WADSWORTH LONGFELLOW.

3. Nature has shown by making it so rare,
That wit's a jewel which we need not *wear*.[2]
— EDWARD YOUNG.

4. Creation's *heir*,[3] the world, the world is mine!
— OLIVER GOLDSMITH.

5. *There*[4] children dwell who know no parents' care;
Parents, who know no children's love, dwell *there*.[4]
GEORGE CRABBE.

1. Copy. 2. Write from dictation, or from memory.

The sea is a jovial comrade;
  He laughs wherever he goes;
His merriment shows in dimpling lines
  That wrinkle his hale repose:
He lays himself down at the feet of the sun,
  And shakes all over with glee;
And the broad-backed billows fall faint on the shore
  In the mirth of the mighty sea.— BAYARD TAYLOR.

LESSON 66.

Flowers.

1. Copy carefully. 2. Write from dictation, or from memory.

1. For the world is full of roses, and the roses full of dew,
   And the dew is full of heavenly love that drips for me and you. — JAMES WHITCOMB RILEY.

2. The jasmine faint, and the sweet tuberose,
   The sweetest flower for scent that blows.
   PERCY BYSSHE SHELLEY.

3. But on the hills the golden-rod, and the aster in the wood,
   And the yellow sunflower by the brook, in Autumn beauty stood. — WILLIAM CULLEN BRYANT.

4. A Sensitive Plant in a garden grew,
   And the young winds fed it with silver dew,
   And it opened its fanlike leaves to the light,
   And closed them beneath the kisses of Night.
   PERCY BYSSHE SHELLEY.

5. The buttercups, bright-eyed and bold,
   Hold up their chalices of gold
   To catch the sunshine and the dew. — JULIA C. R. DORR.

6. The pansy in her purple dress,
   The pink with cheek of red,
   Or the faint, fair heliotrope, who hangs,
   Like a bashful maid, her head. — PHŒBE CARY.

LESSON 67.

Signs used for e as in me.

$\overset{1}{ea}$, $\overset{2}{ee}$, $\overset{3}{ie}$, $\overset{4}{ei}$, $\overset{5}{i}$, $\overset{6}{ey}$, $\overset{7}{eo}$ = $\bar{e}$.

1. Copy the following sentences. 2. Write from dictation.

1. And then *each*[1] pale lily, that slept in the *stream*,[1]
Rose and fell with a wave, as if stirr'd by a *dream*.[1]
— AMELIA B. WELBY.

2. My Mary's *asleep*[2] by thy murmuring *stream*[1] —
Flow gently, *sweet*[2] Afton, disturb not her *dream*.[1]
— ROBERT BURNS.

3. A man who can't put fire into his *speeches*[2] should put his *speeches*[2] into the fire. — WILLIAM MATHEWS.

4. Honest plain words best *pierce*[3] the *ear*[1] of *grief*.[3]
WILLIAM SHAKESPEARE.

5. When honor comes to you be ready to take it;
But *reach*[1] not to *seize*[4] it before it is *near*.[1]
— JOHN BOYLE O'REILLY.

6. The hills we climbed, the river *seen*[2]
By *gleams*[1] along its *deep*[2] *ravine*,[5] —
All *keep*[2] the memory fresh and *green*.[2]
JOHN GREENLEAF WHITTIER.

7. They say he wears a *key*[6] in his *ear*[1] and a lock hanging by it. — WILLIAM SHAKESPEARE.

8. The world *deals*[1] good-naturedly with good-natured *people*.[7] — WILLIAM MAKEPEACE THACKERAY.

9. Government of the *people*,[7] by the *people*,[7] and for the *people*[7] shall not perish from the earth.
— ABRAHAM LINCOLN.

LESSON 68.

Signs used for e as in met.

1 2 3 4 5 6 7 8 9
ĕa, ai, ĕo, a, ĕi, uĕ, iĕ, ay, u = ĕ.

1. Copy the following sentences. 2. Write from dictation.

1. When, even on the mountain's *breast*,[1]
   The chainless winds were all at rest.
   — WILLIAM CULLEN BRYANT.

2. Faith, that's as well *said*[2] as if I had *said*[2] it myself. — JONATHAN SWIFT.

3. Lions make *leopards*[3] tame.
   Yea, but not change his spots. — WILLIAM SHAKESPEARE.

4. A laugh is worth a hundred groans in *any*[4] market.
   — CHARLES LAMB.

5. The *heifer*[5] that lows in the upland farm,
   Far-heard, lows not thine ear to charm.
   — RALPH WALDO EMERSON.

6. I know no cause
   Why I should welcome such a *guest*[6] as grief.
   — WILLIAM SHAKESPEARE.

7. Though old the thought and oft exprest,
   'Tis his at last who *says*[8] it best.
   — JAMES RUSSELL LOWELL.

8. Crush me, ye rocks; ye falling mountains hide,
   Or *bury*[9] me in ocean's angry tide. — WILLIAM COWPER.

9. He who has a thousand *friends*[7] has not a *friend*[7] to spare,
   And he who has one enemy shall meet him everywhere. — ALI BEN ABU TALEB.

LESSON 69.

Flowers.

1. Copy carefully. 2. Write from dictation, or from memory.

1. And queen hollyhocks,
   With butterflies for crowns. — JEAN INGELOW.

2. And honeysuckle loved to crawl
   Up the long crag and ruined wall. — SIR WALTER SCOTT.

3. And the Hyacinth purple, and white, and blue,
   Which flung from its bells a peal anew
   Of music so delicate, soft, and intense,
   It was felt like an odor within the sense.
   — PERCY BYSSHE SHELLEY.

4. Oh, a dainty plant is the ivy green,
   That creepeth o'er ruins old! — CHARLES DICKENS.

5. Open afresh your round of starry folds,
   Ye ardent marigolds. — JOHN KEATS.

6. The morning-glory's blossoming
   Will soon be coming round;
   We see their rows of heart-shaped leaves
   Upspringing from the ground. — MARIA WHITE LOWELL.

7. The thistle's purple bonnet,
   And bonny heather bell,
   Oh, they're the flowers of Scotland
   All others that excel! — JAMES HOGG.

LESSON 70.

Signs used for i as in **pine**.

$\overset{1}{y}, \overset{2}{ie}, \overset{3}{ui}, \overset{4}{ei}, \overset{5}{ye}, \overset{6}{uy}, \overset{7}{ai}, \overset{8}{eye} = \bar{i}.$

1. Copy the following sentences. 2. Write from dictation.

1. To time
The task was left to whittle thee away
With his *sly*[1] *scythe.*[1] — WILLIAM COWPER.

2. What moistens the lips and what brightens the *eye?*[8]
What calls back the past, like the rich pumpkin *pie?*[2]
— JOHN GREENLEAF WHITTIER.

3. The shades of evening *lie*[2]
On Earth and Ocean. — PERCY BYSSHE SHELLEY.

4. There's beauty all around our paths, if but our watchful *eyes*[8]
Can trace it 'midst familiar things, and through their lowly *guise.*[3] — FELICIA D. HEMANS.

5. I see, but cannot reach, the *height*[4]
That *lies*[2] forever in the light.
HENRY WADSWORTH LONGFELLOW.

6. The lily's hue, the rose's *dye,*[5]
The kindling luster of an *eye.*[8] — ROBERT BURNS.

7. Then take what gold could never *buy*[6] —
An honest bard's esteem. — ROBERT BURNS.

8. Here, where the fretted *aisles*[7] prolong
The distant notes of holy song. — SIR WALTER SCOTT.

WASHINGTON IRVING

1783 ⚜ 1859

LESSON 71.

Signs used for i as in **pin**.

ў, uI, ee, e, u, Ie, o = I.
(1, 2, 3, 4, 5, 6, 7)

   1. Copy the following sentences.   2. Write from dictation.

1. The music of the woodland depths, a *hymn*[1]
Of gladness and of thanks. — WILLIAM CULLEN BRYANT.

2. The redbreast loves to *build*[2] and warble there,
And little footprints *lightly*[1] print the ground.
— THOMAS GRAY.

3. Not heaven itself upon the past has power;
But what has *been*[3] has *been*,[3] and I have had my hour. — JOHN DRYDEN.

4. Poor harmless fly,
That, with his *pre⁴tty*[1] buzzing *melody*,[1]
Came here to make us *merry!*[1] — WILLIAM SHAKESPEARE.

5.   Be *England*[4] what she will,
With all her faults, she is my *country*[1] still.
— CHARLES CHURCHILL.

6. Ye lakes whose vessels catch the *busy*[5] gale.
— OLIVER GOLDSMITH.

7. Honor *women!*[7] they entwine and weave *heavenly*[1]
roses in our *earthly*[1] life. — JOHANN C. F. SCHILLER.

8. I pray thee, cease thy counsel,
Which falls into mine ears as profitless
As water in a *sieve*.[6] — WILLIAM SHAKESPEARE.

LESSON 72.

Flowers.

1. Copy carefully. 2. Write from dictation, or from memory.

1. I like the chaliced lilies,
   The heavy Eastern lilies,
   The gorgeous tiger lilies
   That in our garden grow.— Thomas Bailey Aldrich.

2. Or columbines, in purple dressed,
   Nod o'er the ground bird's hidden nest.
   — William Cullen Bryant.

3. Not proudly high, nor meanly low,
   A graceful myrtle rear'd its head.— James Montgomery.

4. Here are sweet peas, on tiptoe for a flight;
   With wings of gentle flush o'er delicate white.
   — John Keats.

5. Her modest looks the cottage might adorn,
   Sweet as the primrose peeps beneath the thorn.
   Oliver Goldsmith.

6. Summer set lip to earth's bosom bare,
   And left the flushed print in a poppy there:
   Like a yawn of fire from the grass it came,
   And the fanning wind puffed it to flapping flame.
   — Francis Thompson.

7. There are no flowers grow in the vale,
   Kiss'd by the dew, woo'd by the gale,
   None by the dew of the twilight wet,
   So sweet as the deep-blue violet.— Letitia E. Landon.

LESSON 73.

Signs used for o as in note.

_{1   2   3   4   5   6   7}
ōa, ōw, ōu, ōe, ōo, ew, eau = ō.

1. Copy the following sentences.   2. Write from dictation.

1.   From the skies
The last red splendor *floats*[1] along my wall
Like a King's banner. — FELICIA D. HEMANS.

2. All things I thought I knew; but now confess
The more I *know*[2] I *know*,[2] I *know*[2] the less.
— DR. JOHN OWEN.

3. O'er the hush'd deep the yellow beam he *throws*,[2]
Gilds the green wave, that trembles as it *glows*.[2]
— GEORGE GORDON, LORD BYRON.

4. The birds *pour*[3] forth their *souls*[3] in notes
Of rapture from a thousand *throats*.[1]
— WILLIAM WORDSWORTH.

5. The waves are singing a song of *woe!*[4]
— JOHN GREENLEAF WHITTIER.

6. Till over the buttons I fall asleep,
And *sew*[6] them on in a dream. — THOMAS HOOD.

7. A lively *beau*[7] of the dapper sort. — JOHN GODFREY SAXE.

8. A *foe*[4] to God was ne'er true friend to man.
EDWARD YOUNG.

9. The whitewash'd wall, the nicely sanded *floor*,[5]
The varnish'd clock that click'd behind the *door*.[5]
— OLIVER GOLDSMITH.

LESSON 76.

Flowers.

1. Copy carefully. 2. Write from dictation, or from memory.

1. Here bloom red roses, dewy wet,
   And beds of fragrant mignonette. — ELAINE GOODALE.

2. Now the tender, sweet arbutus
   Trails her blossom-clustered vines. — DORA R. GOODALE.

3. And in the woods a fragrance rare
   Of wild azaleas fills the air,
   And richly tangled overhead
   We see their blossoms sweet and red.
   DORA R. GOODALE.

4. Hope's gentle gem, the sweet forget-me-not.
   SAMUEL TAYLOR COLERIDGE.

5. Wild rose, sweetbrier, eglantine,
   All these pretty names are mine. — LEIGH HUNT.

6. In matchless beauty, tender and serene,
   The gentian reigned, an undisputed queen.
   — ELAINE GOODALE.

7. O'erhead we see the jasmine, and sweetbrier,
   And bloomy grapes laughing from green attire.
   JOHN KEATS.

8. Would that the little flowers were born to live,
   Conscious of half the pleasure which they give.
   — WILLIAM WORDSWORTH.

LESSON 77.

Signs used for u as in mute.

$$\overset{1}{\text{ew}}, \overset{2}{\text{ue}}, \overset{3}{\text{eu}}, \overset{4}{\text{ui}}, \overset{5}{\text{iew}}, \overset{6}{\text{ieu}}, \overset{7}{\text{eau}} = \bar{\text{u}}.$$

1. Copy the following sentences. 2. Write from dictation.

1. And open pastures, where you scarcely tell
White daisies from white *dew*.[1]
>> ELIZABETH BARRETT BROWNING.

2. Oft to its warbling waters drew
My little feet, when life was *new*.[1]
>> —WILLIAM CULLEN BRYANT.

3. And that was the way
The *deuce*[3] was to pay
As it always is, at the close of the day.
>> — WILL CARLETON.

4. But mark! what arch of varied *hue*[2]
From heaven to earth is bowed?
Haste, ere it vanish! — haste to *view*[5]
The rainbow in the cloud. —FELICIA D. HEMANS.

5. His dress a *suit*[4] of fray'd magnificence.
>> — ALFRED TENNYSON.

6. So sweetly she bade me *adieu*,[6]
I thought that she bade me return.
>> —WILLIAM SHENSTONE.

7. Autumn's earliest frost had given
To the woods below
Hues[2] of *beauty*,[7] such as heaven
Lendeth to its bow. —JOHN GREENLEAF WHITTIER.

LESSON 78.

Signs used for u as in tub.

   1   2   3   4
   ŏ, oŭ, ŏo, ŏe = ŭ.

1. Copy the following sentences.   2. Write from dictation.

1. A finch, whose *tongue*[1] knew no control.
                  — WILLIAM COWPER.

2. The *touch*[2] of the sunbeam hath waked the rose.
                  — FELICIA D. HEMANS.

3. Bliss was it in that dawn to be alive,
But to be *young*[2] was very heaven!
                  — WILLIAM WORDSWORTH.

4. Handsome *enough*,[2] if they be good *enough*;[2] for handsome is that handsome *does*.[4]
                  — OLIVER GOLDSMITH.

5. The *flood*[3] of time is rolling on. — PERCY BYSSHE SHELLEY.

6. The sultry summer day is *done*,[1]
The western hills have hid the sun. — SIR WALTER SCOTT.

Some words pronounced alike

1. Copy carefully.   2. Write from dictation.   3. Use the italicized words in sentences of your own.

1. Rich and rare were the gems she wore,
And a bright gold *ring* on her wand she bore.
                  — THOMAS MOORE.

2. To *wring* from me and tell to them my secret.
                  — JOHN MILTON.

3.   In his noontide bower,
Makes woodland echoes *ring*. — ROBERT BURNS.

GEORGE GORDON, LORD BYRON

1788 ✣ 1824

LESSON 79.

Some words pronounced alike.

1. Copy carefully. 2. Write from dictation. 3. Use the italicized words in sentences of your own.

1.   In that glorious *clime*
Where Nature laughs in scorn of Time.
FELICIA D. HEMANS.

2. From *clime* to *clime* he sped his course.
WILLIAM COWPER.

3. Ah! who can tell how hard it is to *climb*
The steep where Fame's proud temple shines afar!
JAMES BEATTIE.

4. The person whom you favored with a *loan*, if he be a good man, will think himself in your debt after he has paid you. — SIR RICHARD STEELE.

5. In some *lone* isle, or distant northern land.
— ALEXANDER POPE.

6. Charms strike the *sight*, but merit wins the soul.
ALEXANDER POPE.

7. The great sun rises to behold the *sight*.
— HENRY WADSWORTH LONGFELLOW.

8. Those Pyramids shall fall;
Their very *site* shall be forgotten,
As is their builder's name! — PERCY BYSSHE SHELLEY.

9. The devil can *cite* scripture for his purpose.
— WILLIAM SHAKESPEARE.

10. They went and *told* the sexton, and the sexton *tolled* the bell. — THOMAS HOOD.

LESSON 80.

ph or **gh** = **f**.

1. Copy the following sentences. 2. Write from dictation.

1. Sport that wrinkled Care derides,
And *Laughter* holding both his sides. — John Milton.

2. *Laugh* and the world *laughs* with you,
Weep and you weep alone;
For the sad old earth must borrow its mirth,
But has trouble *enough* of its own.
— Ella Wheeler Wilcox.

3. For not an *orphan* in the wide world can be so deserted as the child who is an outcast from a living parent's love. — Charles Dickens.

4. The village all declared how much he knew;
'Twas certain he could write and *cipher*, too.
— Oliver Goldsmith.

5. That very law which molds a tear,
And bids it trickle from its source,
That law preserves the earth a *sphere*,
And guides the planets in their course.
— Samuel Rogers.

6. Of all the horrid, hideous notes of woe,
Sadder than owl-songs or the midnight blast,
Is that portentous *phrase*, "I told you so."
— George Gordon, Lord Byron.

7. There's a divinity that shapes our ends
Rough-hew them how we will. — William Shakespeare.

LESSON 81.

Some words pronounced alike.

1. Copy carefully. 2. Write from dictation. 3. Use the italicized words in sentences of your own.

1. Who hath not saved some trifling thing
   More prized than jewels rare,
   A faded flower, a broken ring,
   A tress of golden *hair*. — ELLEN C. HOWARTH.

2. The merry, merry lark was up and singing,
   And the *hare* was out and feeding on the lea.
   — CHARLES KINGSLEY.

3. Where throngs of *knights* and barons bold
   In weeds of peace high triumphs hold. — JOHN MILTON.

4. 'Tis the witching hour of *night*,
   Orbed is the moon and bright,
   And the stars they glisten, glisten,
   Seeming with bright eyes to listen. — JOHN KEATS.

5. Like some of nature's sweetest flowers,
   Rose from a *seed* of tiny size
   That seemed to promise no such prize.
   — WILLIAM COWPER.

6. The people must *cede* to the government some of their natural rights. — JOHN JAY.

7. To many a youth, and many a *maid*,
   Dancing in the checkered shade. — JOHN MILTON.

8. God *made* the country, and man *made* the town.
   — WILLIAM COWPER.

LESSON 82.

çh soft = sh.

1. Copy the following sentences.   2. Write from dictation.

1.   Or rather dost thou tread
   Those cloudy summits thence to gaze below,
   Like the wild *chamois* from her Alpine snow?
   — THOMAS HOOD.

2.   He steps into the welcome *chaise*,
   Lolls at his ease behind four handsome bays.
   — WILLIAM COWPER.

3. *Charades* and riddles as at Christmas here.
   — ALFRED TENNYSON.

4. For He, who gave this vast *machine* to roll,
   Breathed Life in them, in us a Reasoning Soul.
   — JUVENAL.

Some words pronounced alike.

1. Copy carefully.   2. Write from dictation.   3. Use the italicized words in sentences of your own.

1. Oh, listen! for the *vale* profound
   Is overflowing with the sound. — WILLIAM WORDSWORTH.

2. And "twilight gray" had spread its dusky *veil*.
   WILLIAM WATSON.

3. England may as well *dam* up the waters of the Nile
          with bulrushes as to fetter the step of Freedom.
   LYDIA M. CHILD.

4. Though by whim, envy, or resentment led,
   They *damn* those authors whom they never read.
   — CHARLES CHURCHILL.

LESSON 83.

ch hard = k.

1. Copy the following sentences. 2. Write from dictation.

1.   Girt by many an azure wave
With which the clouds and mountains pave
A lake's blue *chasm*.— PERCY BYSSHE SHELLEY.

2. Nay, in every *epoch* of the world, the great event, parent of all others, is it not the arrival of a Thinker in the world?— THOMAS CARLYLE.

3. Let *echo*, too, perform her part,
Prolonging every note with art.— JOSEPH ADDISON.

4. Whatever makes men good *Christians*, makes them good citizens.— DANIEL WEBSTER.

5. *Character* is formed in the stormy billows of the world.— JOHANN W. GOETHE.

6. The accent, or turn of expression of a single sentence, will at once mark a *scholar*.— JOHN RUSKIN.

7. The mystic *chords* of memory, stretching from every battlefield and patriot grave to every living heart and hearthstone all over this broad land, will yet swell the *chorus* of the Union, when again touched, as surely they will be, by the better angels of our nature.— ABRAHAM LINCOLN.

LESSON 84.

ch unmarked.

1. Copy the following sentences. 2. Write from dictation.

1. An honest man is always a *child*. — MARCUS V. MARTIAL.

2.   The rivers wove their *charms*,
And every little daisy in the grass
Did look up in my face, and smile to see me pass!
        — RICHARD HENRY STODDARD.

3. *Chance* is a word void of sense; nothing can exist without a cause. — VOLTAIRE.

4. 'Tis thus that on the *choice* of friends
Our good or evil name depends. — JOHN GAY.

5. Oft in the stilly night
E'er slumber's *chain* has bound me,
Fond memory brings the light
Of other days around me. — THOMAS MOORE.

6. How can ye *chant*, ye little birds,
And I so weary full of care? — ROBERT BURNS.

7. Happy the *child* who is suffered to be and content to be what God meant it to be — a *child* while *childhood* lasts. — FREDERICK WILLIAM ROBERTSON.

8. The bluebird *chants*, from the elm's long *branches*,
A hymn to welcome the budding year.
        — WILLIAM CULLEN BRYANT.

LESSON 85.

Some words pronounced alike.

1. Copy carefully. 2. Write from dictation. 3. Use the italicized words in sentences of your own.

1. One lone *beech,* unclosing there
   Its light leaves in the vernal air.
   — JOHN GREENLEAF WHITTIER.

2. No sound was heard save the last sob of some retiring wave, telling its story to the smooth pebbles of the *beach.* — ELIJAH KELLOGG.

3. The antlered Monarch of the *waste*
   Sprang from his heathery couch in haste.
   SIR WALTER SCOTT.

4. With all the flowers he found, he wove in haste
   Wreaths for her brow, and girdles for her *waist.*
   — WILLIAM COWPER.

5. Full many a flower is born to blush unseen,
   And *waste* its sweetness on the desert air.
   — THOMAS GRAY.

6. He is the happiest, be he king or peasant, who finds *peace* in his own home. — JOHANN W. GOETHE.

7. I'll make a *piece* of poetry. — BEN JONSON.

8. What a *piece* of work is man! — WILLIAM SHAKESPEARE.

9. *Bread* of flour is good; but there is *bread,* sweet as honey, if we would eat it, in a good book.
   JOHN RUSKIN.

10. He hath never fed of the dainties that are *bred* in a book. — WILLIAM SHAKESPEARE.

LESSON 86.

Surd th as in **thin**, unmarked.

1. Copy the following sentences. 2. Write from dictation.

1. Yet this is Rome,
That sat on her seven hills, and from her *throne*
Of beauty ruled the world. — Mary Russell Mitford.

2. Let us then, be what we are, and speak what we *think*,
And in all *things* keep ourselves loyal to *truth*.
— Henry Wadsworth Longfellow.

3. The primrose opes its eye,
And the young *moth* flutters by. — Eliza Cook.

4. Where the night has its grave and the morning its *birth*. — Percy Bysshe Shelley.

5. Yet oft, in his marble *hearth's* bright glow,
He watch'd a picture come and go.
— John Greenleaf Whittier.

6. The clouds o'er their summits they calmly did rest,
And hung on the *ether's* invisible breast.
John Ruskin.

7. And can it be that in a world so full and busy, the loss of one weak creature makes a void in any heart, so wide and deep that *nothing* but the *width* and *depth* of vast eternity can fill it up!
Charles Dickens.

8. The measure of life is not *length*, but honesty.
— John Lyly.

PERCY BYSSHE SHELLEY

1792 ⚜ 1822

1. Copy carefully.   2. Write from dictation, or from memory.

THE DAFFODILS

I wander'd lonely as a cloud
That floats on high o'er vales and hills,
When all at once I saw a crowd,
A host, of golden daffodils;
Beside the lake, beneath the trees,
Fluttering and dancing in the breeze.

Continuous as the stars that shine
And twinkle on the milky way,
They stretch'd in never-ending line
Along the margin of the bay:
Ten thousand saw I at a glance,
Tossing their heads in sprightly dance.

The waves beside them danced; but they
Outdid the sparkling waves in glee:
A poet could not but be gay,
In such a jocund company:
I gazed — and gazed — but little thought
What wealth the show to me had brought:

For oft, when on my couch I lie
In vacant or in pensive mood,
They flash upon that inward eye
Which is the bliss of solitude;
And then my heart with pleasure fills,
And dances with the daffodils. — WILLIAM WORDSWORTH.

LESSON 88.

Sonant th as in the, marked th̲.

1. Copy the following sentences.   2. Write from dictation.

1. *They* are never alone *that* are accompanied *with* noble thoughts. — Sir Philip Sidney.

2. To *them* his heart, his love, his griefs were given,
But all his serious thoughts had rest in heaven.
— Oliver Goldsmith.

3. How beautiful *the* silent hour, when morning and evening *thus* sit *together*, hand in hand, beneath *the* starless sky of midnight!
— Henry Wadsworth Longfellow.

4. Night drew her sable curtain down
And pinned it *with* a star. — M'Donald Clarke.

5. Vapors *clothe* earth's monarch mountain-tops
With kingly ermine snow. — Percy Bysshe Shelley.

6. Oh! but to *breathe the* breath
Of *the* cowslip and primrose sweet —
With the sky above my head,
And *the* grass beneath my feet! — Thomas Hood.

7. We did so laugh and cry *with* you,
I've half a mind to die *with* you,
Old year, if you must die. — Alfred Tennyson.

8. *Hither* and *thither with* screams as wild
As the laughing mirth of a rosy child. — Mary Howitt.

LESSON 89.
Some words pronounced alike.

1. Copy carefully. 2. Write from dictation. 3. Use the italicized words in sentences of your own.

1. O, rivers, forests, hills, and plains!
   Oft have ye *heard* my merry strains. — ROBERT BURNS.

2. The fall of waters, and the song of birds,
   And the hills that echo to the distant *herds*.
   — WILLIAM COWPER.

3. But far more numerous was the *herd* of such,
   Who think too little and who talk too much.
   JOHN DRYDEN.

4. The miser's *sum* of happiness is, always, — addition.
   — FREDERICK SAUNDERS.

5. Muttering thunder *some* sad drops wept.
   JOHN MILTON

6. *Sum* up at night what thou hast done by day;
   And in the morning what thou hast to do.
   GEORGE HERBERT.

7. Trifles make the *sum* of human things.
   — HANNAH MORE.

8. Like the *scent* of a flower in its folded bell,
   When eve through the woodlands hath sighed farewell.— FELICIA D. HEMANS.

9. Millions for defense, but not one *cent* for tribute.
   — CHARLES C. PINCKNEY.

10. O Scotia! my dear, my native soil!
    For whom my warmest wish to heaven is *sent!*
    — ROBERT BURNS.

LESSON 90.

Sound of n like ng, marked ṇ.

1. Copy the following sentences. 2. Write from dictation.

1.   A small drop of *ink*,
Falling like dew, upon a thought produces
That which makes thousands, perhaps millions, *think*.
                        — GEORGE GORDON, LORD BYRON.

2. Modern poets mix too much water with their *ink*.
                        JOHANN W. GOETHE.

3. How few *think* justly of the *thinking* few!
How many never *think*, who *think* they do.
                        — JANE TAYLOR.

4. At Learning's fountain it is sweet to *drink*,
But 'tis a nobler privilege to *think*.
                        JOHN GODFREY SAXE.

5. Sweet Morn, I *thank* thee for thy sunny beams.
                        — WILLIAM SHAKESPEARE.

6. Rose! thou art the sweetest flower,
That ever *drank* the amber shower. — THOMAS MOORE.

7. The *twinkling* stars began to muster,
And glitter with their borrowed luster.
                        — SAMUEL BUTLER.

8. Roll on, thou deep and dark blue Ocean — roll! . .
Time writes no *wrinkle* on thine azure brow —
Such as creation's dawn beheld, thou rollest now.
                        — GEORGE GORDON, LORD BYRON.

9. The flood of time is rolling on;
We stand upon its *brink*. — PERCY BYSSHE SHELLEY.

LESSON 91.

qu = kw.

1. Copy the following sentences. 2. Write from dictation.

1. When the pebble-paven shore,
   Under the *quick* faint kisses of the sea
   Trembles and sparkles with ecstasy.
   — PERCY BYSSHE SHELLEY.

2. He hath a killing tongue and a *quiet* sword.
   — WILLIAM SHAKESPEARE.

3. And bear unmov'd the wrongs of base mankind,
   The last, and hardest, *conquest* of the mind. — HOMER.

4. Does the *quail* sit up and whistle in a disappointed way?
   Or hang his head in silence and sorrow all the day?
   — JAMES WHITCOMB RILEY.

5. A *quarrel* is *quickly* settled when deserted by one party: there is no battle unless there are two.
   — SENECA.

6. "Thanks!" said the Judge; "a sweeter draught
   From a fairer hand was never *quaff'd*."
   — JOHN GREENLEAF WHITTIER.

7. As soon go kindle fire with snow
   As seek to *quench* the fire of love with words.
   WILLIAM SHAKESPEARE.

8. There was tumult in the city,
   In the *quaint* old *Quaker* town. — ANON.

9. Then doth thy sweet and *quiet* eye
   Look through its fringes to the sky.
   — WILLIAM CULLEN BRYANT.

LESSON 94.

Some words pronounced alike.

1. Copy carefully.   2. Write from dictation.   3. Use the italicized words in sentences of your own.

1. With common wants and common cares,
   Which sow the human heart with *tares*.
   — PERCY BYSSHE SHELLEY.

2. I am not mad: this hair I *tear* is mine.
   WILLIAM SHAKESPEARE.

3. Everything comes if a man will only *wait*.
   — BENJAMIN DISRAELI.

4. Nor lift your load before you're quite aware
   What *weight* your shoulders will, or will not, bear.
   GEORGE GORDON, LORD BYRON.

5. The thirsty earth soaks up the *rain*. — ABRAHAM COWLEY.

6. As when Night is bare
   From one lonely cloud
   The moon *rains* out her beams, and Heaven is overflowed. — PERCY BYSSHE SHELLEY.

7. Into each life some *rain* must fall,
   Some days must be dark and dreary.
   — HENRY WADSWORTH LONGFELLOW.

8. My tongue within my lips I *rein*,
   For who talks much, must talk in vain. — JOHN GAY.

9. The queen of night asserts her silent *reign*.
   GEORGE GORDON, LORD BYRON.

LESSON 95.

$$\overset{1}{s},\ \overset{2}{si},\ \overset{3}{sci},\ \overset{4}{ci},\ \text{or}\ \overset{5}{ti} = sh.$$

1. Copy carefully.   2. Write from dictation.

1. As *sure*[1] as I have a thought or a soul.
— WILLIAM SHAKESPEARE.

2. Around it still the *sumacs*[1] grow,
And blackberry vines are running.
— JOHN GREENLEAF WHITTIER.

3. Yet e'en this cheerless *mansion*[2] shall provide
More heart's repose than all the world beside.
— LEONIDAS.

4. Nothing makes the earth seem so *spacious*[4] as to have friends at a distance; they make the latitude and longitude. — HENRY DAVID THOREAU.

5. Some *circumstantial*[5] evidence is very strong, as when you find a trout in the milk.
HENRY DAVID THOREAU.

6. See what a ready tongue *suspicion*[4] hath!
— WILLIAM SHAKESPEARE.

7. He builded better than he knew:
The *conscious*[3] stone to beauty grew.
— RALPH WALDO EMERSON.

8. *Gracious*[4] as sunshine, sweet as dew.
— MARGARET J. PRESTON.

9. Think that day lost whose low descending sun
Views from thy hand no noble *action*[5] done.
JACOB BOBART.

10. All hush'd — there's not a breeze in *motion;*[5]
The shore is silent as the ocean. — THOMAS MOORE.

LESSON 96.

Some words pronounced alike.

1. Copy carefully.   2. Write from dictation.   3. Use the italicized words in sentences of your own.

1. Hunting the *hart* in forest green. — SIR WALTER SCOTT.

2. Absence makes the *heart* grow fonder.
— THOMAS HAYNES BAYLY.

3. Life! we've been long together
 Through pleasant and *through* cloudy weather.
ANNA L. BARBAULD.

4. And stately oaks their twisted arms,
 Threw broad and dark across the pool.
— ROBERT BURNS.

5. As creeping ivy clings to *wood* or stone,
 And hides the ruin that it feeds upon.
— WILLIAM COWPER.

6. I *would* you were as I *would* have you be!
 Would it be better, madam, than I am?
— WILLIAM SHAKESPEARE.

7. Every pine and *fir* and hemlock
 Wore ermine too dear for an earl.
JAMES RUSSELL LOWELL.

8. Nature's children all divide her care,
 The *fur* that warms a monarch warmed a bear.
— ALEXANDER POPE.

9. These all in sweet confusion sought the shade,
 And fill'd each *pause* the nightingale had made.
— OLIVER GOLDSMITH.

10. Devouring Time, blunt thou the lion's *paws*.
WILLIAM SHAKESPEARE.

LESSON 97.

Long a preserved in syllables without accent, marked å.

   1. Copy the following sentences.   2. Write from dictation.

1. Gently on tiptoe *Sunday* creeps,
   Cheerfully from the stars he peeps,
   Mortals are all asleep below,
   None in the *village* hears him go. — JOHN PETER HEBEL.

2. *Thursday* come, and the week is gone.
   — GEORGE HERBERT.

3. The world goes up and the world goes down.
   And the sunshine follows the rain;
   And *yesterday's* sneer and *yesterday's* frown
   Can never come over again. — CHARLES KINGSLEY.

4. With equal pace, impartial Fate
   Knocks at the *palace*, as the *cottage* gate. — HORACE.

5. The moon's fair *image* quaketh
   In the raging waves of ocean;
   While she, in the vault of heaven,
   Moves with silent peaceful motion. — HEINRICH HEINE.

6. The sun can *image* itself in a tiny dewdrop or in the mighty ocean. — RICHARD C. TRENCH.

7. Suspicion *always* haunts the guilty mind.
   — WILLIAM SHAKESPEARE.

LESSON 98.

Long e preserved in syllables without accent, marked ē.

1. Copy the following sentences. 2. Write from dictation.

1. I care not, Fortune, what you me *deny;*
   You cannot rob me of free Nature's grace,
   You cannot shut the windows of the sky,
   Through which Aurora shows her brightening face.
   — JAMES THOMSON.

2. We hold these truths to be self-evident, — that all men are *created* equal. — THOMAS JEFFERSON.

3.   Nature never did *betray*
   The heart that loved her. — WILLIAM WORDSWORTH.

4. Fancy shall weave a charm for my *relief.*
   WILLIAM COWPER.

5. But see, the shepherds shun the noonday heat,
   The lowing herds to murmuring brooks *retreat.*
   — ALEXANDER POPE.

6. Out upon Time! who forever will leave
   But *enough* of the past for the future to grieve.
   — GEORGE GORDON, LORD BYRON.

7. *Behavior* is a mirror in which every one shows his image. — JOHANN W. GOETHE.

8.   Echo *replies,*
   As if another chase were in the skies.
   WILLIAM SHAKESPEARE.

9. The tides of Music's golden sea
   Setting toward *eternity.* — ALFRED TENNYSON.

LESSON 99.

Long o preserved in syllables without accent, marked ȯ.

1. Copy the following sentences.   2. Write from dictation.

1. If *hero* means sincere man, why may not every one of us be a *hero?* — Thomas Carlyle.

2. O for a seat in some *poetic* nook,
Just hid with trees, and sparkling with a brook!
— Leigh Hunt.

3. Would you know what money is? Go *borrow* some.
— George Herbert.

4. O beautiful rainbow, — all woven of light!
There's not in thy tissue one *shadow* of night.
— Sarah J. Hale.

5. No more the flow'r in field or *meadow* springs;
No more the grove with airy concert rings.
— Robert Burns.

6. Winds wander, and dews drip earthward,
Rain falls, suns rise and set,
Earth whirls, and all but to prosper
A poor little *violet.* — James Russell Lowell.

7. I sat by my *window* one night,
And watched how the stars grew high;
And the earth and sky were a splendid sight
To a sober and musing eye.
— Henry Wadsworth Longfellow.

8.   Some dead lake
That holds the *shadow* of a lark
Hung in the *shadow* of a heaven. — Alfred Tennyson.

LESSON 100.

Long ĭ and ŭ preserved in syllables without accent, marked ĭ, ŭ.

1. Copy the following sentences. 2. Write from dictation.

1. He who comes up to his own *idea* of greatness, must always have had a very low standard of it in his mind. — WILLIAM HAZLITT.

2. O let us still the secret joy partake,
   To follow *virtue* even for *virtue's* sake.
   — ALEXANDER POPE.

3. Men are seldom blest with good *fortune* and good sense at the same time. — LIVY.

4. *Nature*, exerting an unwearied power,
   Forms, opens, and gives scent to every flower.
   — WILLIAM COWPER.

5. The *picture* must not be overbright,
   Yet all in the golden and gracious light
   Of a cloud, when the summer sun is down.
   ALICE CARY.

6. Man passes away; his name perishes from record and recollection; his history is as a tale that is told, and his very *monument* becomes a ruin.
   — WASHINGTON IRVING.

7. "There's nothing," said Toby, "more *regular* in its coming round than dinner-time, and nothing less *regular* in its coming round than dinner."
   CHARLES DICKENS.

8. *Nature* sleeps in the plant, dreams in the animal, wakes in the man. — FRIEDRICH W. J. SCHELLING.

LESSON 101.

Some words pronounced alike.

1. Copy carefully. 2. Write from dictation. 3. Use the italicized words in sentences of your own.

1. Boatman, come, thy *fare* receive;
   Thrice thy *fare* I gladly give. — JOHANN LUDWIG UHLAND.

2. When purple morning starts the hare,
   To steal upon her early *fare*. — ROBERT BURNS.

3. Her eyes were *fair* and very *fair*;
   Her beauty made me glad. — WILLIAM WORDSWORTH.

4.   The juicy *pear*
   Lies, in soft profusion, scattered round.
                                   — JAMES THOMSON.

5. Age and Want, oh! ill-matched *pair!* — ROBERT BURNS.

6. He *pares* his apple that will cleanly feed.
                                   — GEORGE HERBERT.

7. All creatures look to the *main* chance.
                                 — SIR ROGER L'ESTRANGE.

8. Each wave was crested with tawny foam,
   Like the *mane* of a chestnut steed. — SIR WALTER SCOTT.

9. Tell how many beads there are
   In a silver chain
   Of evening rain
   Unraveled from the trembling *main*.
                               THOMAS LOVELL BEDDOES.

LESSON 102.

Definitions.

A **Vowel** is a letter which represents a sound of the human voice but slightly interrupted by the vocal organs.

The vowels are *a, e, i, o, u,* and sometimes *w* and *y*. *w* and *y* are consonants at the beginning of a word or a syllable; as in wet, yet; they are vowels in cow, dying, duty, etc.

A **Consonant** is a letter which represents a sound of the human voice greatly obstructed by the organs of speech.

A **Diphthong** is a union of two vowel sounds pronounced in one syllable; as, *ou* in *out*.

A **Triphthong** is a union of three vowels in the same syllable; as, *eau* in *beau*.

A **Digraph** is two vowels or two consonants combined to express a single sound; as, *ea* in *head*, or *th* in *both*.

A **Syllable** is one or more letters pronounced by a single effort of the voice.

A **Monosyllable** is a word of one syllable; as, *class*.

A **Dissyllable** is a word of two syllables; as, *class ing*.

A **Trisyllable** is a word of three syllables; as, *clas si fy*.

A **Polysyllable** is a word of more than three syllables; as, *clas si fy ing* or *clas si fi ca tion*.

Accent is stress of voice on a particular syllable of a word.

A **Prefix** is one or more letters or syllables placed *before* a word to qualify its meaning; as, *un* in *un*kind.

A **Suffix** is one or more letters or syllables placed *after* a word to qualify its meaning; as, *ly* in man*ly*.

A **Primitive** word is one not derived from another word in the same language; as, *man*.

A **Derivative** word is one formed from another word; as, *manly*.

A **Compound** word is one composed of two or more simple words; as, *inkstand, to-day*.

RALPH WALDO EMERSON

1803 ✤ 1882

LESSON 103.

Rules for Spelling.

The value of the Rules for Spelling will depend much upon the pupil's familiarity with the exceptions. These exceptions are really very few when compared with the thousands of words controlled by the Rules.

Rule I. Most words ending in silent *e* drop the *e* before a suffix beginning with a *vowel*.

>EXAMPLE: choose, choosing; change, changing.

Be slow in *choosing* a friend, slower in *changing*.
— BENJAMIN FRANKLIN.

Exceptions to Rule I.

Some words ending in *e* retain the *e* before a suffix beginning with a *vowel,* to prevent a change in pronunciation, or to preserve the identity of the word.

hoe ing	free ing	tinge ing	trace a ble
shoe ing	see ing	cringe ing	no tice a ble
toe ing	dye ing	change a ble	peace a ble
flee ing	singe ing	a gree a ble	mile age

It is inferred from Rule I. that *e* is not dropped before a suffix beginning with a *consonant,* but the following are exceptions:

aw ful	whol ly	judg ment	nurs ling
du ly	wo ful	lodg ment	a bridg ment
tru ly	wis dom	ar gu ment	ac knowl edg ment

Next to sound *judgment,* diamonds and pearls are the rarest things to be met with. — DE LA BRUYERE.

LESSON 104.

Some words pronounced alike.

1. Copy carefully. 2. Write from dictation. 3. Use the italicized words in sentences of your own.

1. From the blue rim, where skies and mountains *meet*,
   Down to the very turf beneath my feet,
   Ten thousand charms. — WILLIAM COWPER.

2. Not the *meat*, but appetite
   Makes our eating a delight. — ROBERT BURNS.

3. It was *meet* that we should make merry. — BIBLE.

4. For with the same measure that ye *mete* withal, it
   shall be measured to you again. — BIBLE.

5. All-cheering Plenty, with her flowing horn,
   Led yellow Autumn wreath'd with nodding corn.
   — ROBERT BURNS.

6. Sure if they cannot cut, it may be said
   His saws are toothless, and his hatchets *lead*.
   — ALEXANDER POPE.

7. There was one song, among the *rest*,
   Above them all it pleas'd me best. — ROBERT BURNS.

8. And the soft breeze from the west
   Scarcely broke their dreamy *rest*.
   JOHN GREENLEAF WHITTIER.

9. *Wrest* from the unwilling earth his luxuries.
   — PERCY BYSSHE SHELLEY.

LESSON 105.

Rules for Spelling.

Rule II. In monosyllables and words accented on the last syllable, a final consonant after a single vowel doubles before a suffix beginning with a vowel (*x*, *k*, and *v* are never doubled).

> EXAMPLES: bud, bud ding; pre fer, pre fer red.

While I *nodded*, nearly *napping*,
Suddenly there came a *tapping*,
As of some one gently *rapping*,
Rapping at my chamber door. — EDGAR ALLAN POE.

While Twilight's curtain gathering far
Is *pinned* with a single diamond star.
M'DONALD CLARKE.

As when the *setting* sun has given
Ten thousand hues to summer even. — SIR WALTER SCOTT.

Exceptions to Rule II.

The final consonant is not doubled when, in the derivative, the accent is thrown from the last syllable of the primitive; as prefer', pref'er ence; refer', ref'er ence. But we have ex cel', ex'cel lent, ex'cel lence. Learn to spell the following words.

gas'es	gas'sy	def'er ence	pref'er a ble
gas'e ous	con'fer ence	in'fer ence	trans fer'a ble

(Why are *l*, *r*, and *t* not doubled in the following words?)

| re vealed | of fered | lim it ed | slum ber ing |

LESSON 106.

Some words pronounced alike.

1. Copy carefully. 2. Write from dictation. 3. Use the italicized words in sentences of your own.

1. The rugged trees are mingling
   Their flowery sprays in love;
   The ivy climbs the laurel
   To clasp the *boughs* above.— WILLIAM CULLEN BRYANT.

2. A compliment is usually accompanied with a *bow*, as if to beg pardon for paying it.
   J. C. AND A. W. HARE.

3. Gracefully, gracefully glides our bark
   On the bosom of Father Thames,
   And before her *bows* the wavelets dark
   Break into a thousand gems.— THOMAS NOEL.

4. I *owed* a trifle, and have paid the debt.
   WILLIAM COWPER.

5. Once more I'll read the *ode* that I have writ.
   — WILLIAM SHAKESPEARE.

6. And lovely is the silvery *scene*.
   When faint the sunbeams smile.— ROBERT SOUTHEY.

7. Doth not my wit become me rarely?
   It is not *seen* enough, you should wear it in your cap.
   — WILLIAM SHAKESPEARE.

8. In every *scene* some moral let it teach,
   And, if it can, at once both please and preach.
   — ALEXANDER POPE.

LESSON 107.

Rules for Spelling.

Rule III. Words ending in *y* preceded by a *consonant* retain the *y* on taking a suffix beginning with *i*; but on taking a suffix beginning *with any other letter*, *y* is in most cases changed to *i*; as cry, crying; glory, glorious; fancy, fanciful. The exceptions are, pity, piteous; duty, duteous; plenty, plenteous; beauty, beauteous. In these words *y* is changed to *e*. *Y* does not change before 's, as: baby, baby's; lady, lady's; enemy, enemy's.

That *beauteous* head, if it did go down,
Carried sunshine into the sea. — ALICE CARY.

A *baby's* feet, like seashells pink.
— ALGERNON CHARLES SWINBURNE.

Words ending in *y* preceded by a *vowel* retain *y* on taking any suffix; as, joy, joyful; valley, valleys. The exceptions are day, daily; lay, laid; pay, paid; say, said.

Most *joyful* let the Poet be;
It is through him that all men see.
— WILLIAM E. CHANNING.

Adjectives of one syllable ending in *y* preceded by a *consonant* retain the *y* on taking any suffix; as, shy, shyly, shyness; sly, slyly, slyness; dry, dryly, dryness. The exceptions are -er, -est; dry, drier, driest, slier, flier.

When the head is held too high
The brains inside are poor and *dry*. — FROM THE GERMAN.

LESSON 108.

Some words pronounced alike.

1. Copy carefully. 2. Write from dictation. 3. Use the italicized words in sentences of your own.

1. Some write their wrongs in marble: he more just,
   Stoop'd down serene and *wrote* them in the dust.
   —SAMUEL MADDEN.

2. Words learned by *rote* a parrot may rehearse,
   But talking is not always to converse.
   WILLIAM COWPER.

3. Just *earns* a scanty pittance, and at night,
   Lies down secure, her heart and pocket light.
   WILLIAM COWPER.

4. When Venus, throned in clouds of rosy hue,
   Flings from her golden *urn* the vesper dew.
   —THOMAS CAMPBELL.

5. Time but th' impression stronger makes,
   As streams their channels deeper *wear*.
   —ROBERT BURNS.

6. King was a name too proud for man to *wear*
   With modesty and meekness.—WILLIAM COWPER.

7. Could doff at ease his scholar's gown
   To peddle *wares* from town to town.
   JOHN GREENLEAF WHITTIER.

8. Or drop and break his master's *plate*.
   —PERCY BYSSHE SHELLEY.

9. The *plaits* and foldings of the drapery.
   —JOSEPH ADDISON.

10. 'Tis *plate* of rare device.—WILLIAM SHAKESPEARE.

LESSON 109.

Rules for Spelling—*ie* and *ei*.

Rule. *i* before *e*
Except after *c*,
Or when sounded as *a*,
As in neighbor and weigh.—Dr. Brewer.

We are slow to *believe* what if *believed* would hurt our feelings.—Ovid.

I've never any pity for *conceited* people, because I think they carry their comfort about with them.
—George Eliot.

Hast thou ever *weigh'd* a sigh?
Or studied the philosophy of tears?—Edward Young.

Learn the simple, rhyming rule given above, and the following most common exceptions: either, neither, leisure, inveigle, seine, seize, weird, heifer, sleight, height, forfeit, surfeit, foreign, sovereign, counterfeit, mullein.

Real happiness is cheap enough, yet how dearly we pay for its *counterfeit*.—Hosea Ballou.

How has he the *leisure* to be sick
In such a justling time?—William Shakespeare

The rose has taken off her robe of red—
The *mullein*-stalk its yellow stars has lost.—Alice Cary.

Men are *neither* suddenly rich nor suddenly good.
—Libanius.

LESSON 110.

Some words pronounced alike.

1. Copy carefully. 2. Write from dictation. 3. Use the italicized words in sentences of your own.

1. Bright gem instinct with music, vocal spark;
   The happiest bird that sprang out of the *ark*.
   —WILLIAM WORDSWORTH.

2. The pale *arc* of the Northern Lights
   Rose o'er the mountain summits.
   —JOHN GREENLEAF WHITTIER.

3. On twigs of hawthorn he regaled,
   On pippins' russet *peel*.—WILLIAM COWPER.

4. I hear the bell's melodious din,
   I hear the organ *peal* within.
   HENRY WADSWORTH LONGFELLOW.

5. Not yet the hawthorn bore her *berries* red.
   WILLIAM COWPER.

6. Ah, well! for us all some sweet hope lies
   Deeply *buried* from human eyes.
   —JOHN GREENLEAF WHITTIER.

7. When grass is chill with rain or dew,
   Beneath my shade, the mother *ewe*
   Lies with her infant lamb.—WILLIAM WORDSWORTH.

8. If he had been as *you* and *you* as he
   You would have slipt like him.—WILLIAM SHAKESPEARE.

9. All green was banished save of pine and *yew*.
   —GEORGE CRABBE.

NATHANIEL HAWTHORNE

1804 — 1864

LESSON 111.

Formation of the plural of nouns.

The plural form of a noun is regularly made by adding *s* to the singular; as, tree, trees; pen, pens; book, books; bird, birds.

> Such a starved bank of moss
>   Till, that May-morn,
> Blue ran the flash across:
>   *Violets* were born! — ROBERT BROWNING.

> Again the *blackbirds* sing; the *streams*
> Wake, laughing, from their winter *dreams,*
> And tremble in the April *showers*
> The *tassels* of the maple *flowers.*
> —JOHN GREENLEAF WHITTIER.

When a noun ends in silent *e* preceded by the sound of *ch, j, s,* or *z,* the addition of *s* increases the number of syllables; as, niche, niches; judge, judges; cage, cages; face, faces; horse, horses; rose, roses.

> Two *roses* on one slender spray
> In sweet communion grew,
> Together hailed the morning ray
> And drank the evening dew. — JAMES MONTGOMERY.

When a noun ends with *ch, s, sh, x,* or *z,* the plural is formed by adding the syllable *es* to the singular; as, church, churches; gas, gases; fish, fishes; box, boxes.

> Where *peaches* glow with sunny dyes
> Like maidens' cheeks when *blushes* rise. — JOHN GAY.

LESSON 112.

Some words pronounced alike.

1. Copy carefully. 2. Write from dictation. 3. Use the italicized words in sentences of your own.

1. The *doe* awoke, and to the lawn,
   Begemm'd with dewdrops, led her fawn.
   —Sir Walter Scott.

2. Smith, cobbler, joiner, he that plies the shears,
   And he that kneads the *dough*. —William Cowper.

3. The golden hours, on angel wings,
   Flew o'er me. —Robert Burns.

4.   Drove his heel into the smolder'd log,
   That sent a blast of sparkles up the *flue*.
   —Alfred Tennyson.

5.   And now can never mourn
   A heart *grown* cold, a head *grown* gray in vain.
   —Percy Bysshe Shelley.

6. Beneath the blasts the leafless forests *groan*.
   —Robert Burns.

7. There were *no* stars — *no* earth, *no* time —
   No check — *no* change — *no* good — *no* crime —
   But silence and a stirless breath
   Which neither was of life nor death.
   —George Gordon, Lord Byron.

8. To *know* that we *know* what we *know*, and that we do not *know* what we do not *know*, that is true knowledge. —Confucius.

LESSON 113.

Formation of the plural of nouns.

Some nouns ending with *f* or *fe* form the plural by adding *s*, while others change *f* into *v* and add *es*.

Add s

chief	fife	gulf	reef	strife
cuff	grief	proof	safe	waif
dwarf	hoof	roof	scarf	serf

If our inward *griefs* were seen written on our brow,
How many would be pitied who are envied now!
— METASTASIO.

Change f into v and add es

leaf	life	elf	wife	shelf
loaf	wolf	self	thief	calf
knife	sheaf	beef	half	wharf (or s)

Boughs are daily rifled
By the gusty *thieves*,
And the book of Nature
Getteth short of *leaves*. — THOMAS HOOD.

October weaves
Rainbows of the forest *leaves*. — LUCY LARCOM.

It was Autumn, and incessant
Piped the quails from shocks and *sheaves*,
And, like living coals, the apples
Burned among the withering *leaves*.
— HENRY WADSWORTH LONGFELLOW.

LESSON 114.

Some words pronounced alike.

1. Copy carefully. 2. Write from dictation. 3. Use the italicized words in sentences of your own.

1. The *sea*! the *sea*! the open *sea*!
   The blue, the fresh, the ever free!
   — BRYAN WALLER PROCTER.

2. *See* Nature gay as when she first began,
   With smiles alluring her admirer, man;
   She spreads the morning over eastern hills,
   Earth glitters with the drops the night distills.
   — WILLIAM COWPER.

3. Winding slow through bush and brake
   Links together lake and lake.
   — HENRY WADSWORTH LONGFELLOW.

4. A *lynx* crouched watchfully among its caves
   And craggy shores. — PERCY BYSSHE SHELLEY.

5. Those happy climes that *lie*
   Where day never shuts his eye. — JOHN MILTON.

6. Barrels of ashes stood by,
   Wood-ashes for leaching the *lye*,
   Parent of home-made soap. — FRANCIS ANDREW MARCH.

7. And, of all *lies* (be that one poet's boast),
   The *lie* that flatters I abhor the most.
   — WILLIAM COWPER.

LESSON 115.

Formation of the plural of nouns.

When a noun ends with *o* preceded by a *vowel*, the plural is formed by adding *s* to the singular; as, folio, folios; ratio, ratios; cameo, cameos; studio, studios.

Some nouns ending with *o* preceded by a *consonant*, form the plural by adding *s*, while others add *es*, but without increasing the number of syllables; as, alto, altos; canto, cantos; potato, potatoes; tomato, tomatoes. Write the plural forms of the following nouns:

Add *s*

Zero, cuckoo, domino, solo, piano, lasso, proviso, bamboo, kangaroo, quarto, memento, soprano, halo, two.

> Hark, how the jolly *cuckoos* sing
> "Cuckoo!" to welcome in the spring.—John Lyly.

Add *es*

Cargo, hero, veto, tornado, grotto, buffalo, echo, motto, volcano, calico, torpedo, fresco, embargo, negro, desperado, mulatto, mosquito.

> Children fill the groves with *echoes* of their glee.
> —William Cullen Bryant.

Spell the following words with one *l* only:—

Until, always, also, almost, already, welcome, belfry, welfare, balance, diligent, altogether, military.

> And, *balancing* on a blackberry-brier,
> The bobolink sang with his heart on fire. —Anon.

LESSON 116

Some words pronounced alike.

1. Copy carefully.   2. Write from dictation.   3. Use the italicized words in sentences of your own.

1. Over his head beholds
A dewy cloud, and in the cloud a *bow*.—JOHN MILTON.

2. Teach infant cheeks a hidden blush to know,
And little hearts to flutter at a *beau*.—ALEXANDER POPE.

3. And the Sabbath *bell*
That over wood and wild and mountain dell
Wanders so far.—SAMUEL ROGERS.

4. Where none admire, 'tis useless to excel;
Where none are beaux, 'tis vain to be a *belle*.
—LORD GEORGE LYTTLETON.

5. Yet Folly ever has a vacant *stare*,
A simpering countenance, and a trifling air.
—WILLIAM COWPER.

6. And in the hush that followed the prayer,
Was heard the old clock on the *stair*.
—HENRY WADSWORTH LONGFELLOW.

7. There's music in the sighing of a *reed;*
There's music in the gushing of a rill.
—GEORGE GORDON, LORD BYRON.

8. In nature's infinite book of secrecy
A little I can *read*.—WILLIAM SHAKESPEARE.

LESSON 117.

Formation of the plural of nouns.

When a noun ends with *y* preceded by a *vowel*, the plural is formed by adding *s*; as, boy, boys; key, keys; toy, toys; valley, valleys.

Remember'd *joys* are never past. — James Montgomery.

When a noun ends with *y* preceded by a *consonant*, the plural is formed by changing *y* into *i* and adding *es*, but without increasing the number of syllables; as, lily, lilies; daisy, daisies; duty, duties.

But who will watch my *lilies*,
When their blossoms open white?
By day the sun shall be sentry,
And the moon and stars by night! — Bayard Taylor.

The dances ended, all the fairy train
For pinks and *daisies* search'd the flow'ry plain.
— Alexander Pope.

Some nouns have the same form in both singular and plural; as, sheep, deer, swine, trout.

Some nouns have two plural forms; as, brother, brothers, brethren; penny, pennies, pence.

The plural of some nouns is formed quite irregularly; as, man, men; woman, women; child, children; foot, feet; goose, geese; tooth, teeth; ox, oxen; louse, lice; mouse, mice.

Men are but *children* of a larger growth. — John Dryden.

LESSON 118.

Some words pronounced alike.

1. Copy carefully. 2. Write from dictation. 3. Use the italicized words in sentences of your own.

1. If Happiness have not her seat
   And center in the breast,
   We may be wise, or rich, or *great*,
   But never can be blest. — ROBERT BURNS.

2. I had rather hear a brazen canstick turn'd,
   Or a dry wheel *grate* on the axle-tree;
   And that would set my teeth nothing on edge,
   Nothing so much as mincing poetry.
   — WILLIAM SHAKESPEARE.

3. Slow broke the gray cold morning; again the sunshine fell,
   Flecked with the shade of bar and *grate*, within my lonely cell. — JOHN GREENLEAF WHITTIER.

4. The moonlit skater's keen delight,
   The *sleigh*-drive through the frosty night.
   JOHN GREENLEAF WHITTIER.

5. Though he *slay* me, yet will I trust him. — BIBLE.

6. We do not what we *ought*,
   What we *ought* not, we do. — MATTHEW ARNOLD.

7. Unfaith in *aught* is want of faith in all.
   ALFRED TENNYSON.

HENRY WADSWORTH LONGFELLOW

1807 ⁂ 1882

LESSON 119.

A useful suffix.

'*s* or ' means *belonging to* or *possession;* as, boy'*s*, *belonging to* a boy; boys', *belonging to* boys.

Singular.

Rule. 1. Write the singular form of the noun. 2. Add the apostrophe. 3. Add *s*.

1. Copy carefully. 2. Write from dictation.

1. *Time's* ruin, *beauty's* wreck, and grim *care's* reign.
— WILLIAM SHAKESPEARE.

2. I hear the whispering voice of Spring,
The *thrush's* trill, the *cat-bird's* cry.
— OLIVER WENDELL HOLMES.

3. Learn not only by the *comet's* rush,
But a *rose's* birth. — ROBERT BROWNING.

4. We shall lack alone
Woman's smile and *girlhood's* beauty,
Childhood's lisping tone. — JOHN GREENLEAF WHITTIER.

Plural.

Rule. 1. Write the plural form of the noun. 2. Add the apostrophe only. 3. Add *s* if the plural does not end in *s*.

1. A tender smile, our *sorrows'* only balm.
— EDWARD YOUNG.

2. Whisperings from the wildwood come,
Mayflowers' breath, and *insects'* hum. — LUCY LARCOM.

3. The image of *men's* wit and knowledge remains in books. — FRANCIS BACON.

LESSON 120.

1. Copy carefully. 2. Write from dictation, or from memory.

I chatter over stony ways,
   In little sharps and trebles,
I bubble into eddying bays,
   I babble on the pebbles.

*   *   *   *

I wind about, and in and out,
   With here a blossom sailing,
And here and there a lusty trout,
   And here and there a grayling.

*   *

I steal by lawns and grassy plots,
   I slide by hazel covers;
I move the sweet forget-me-nots
   That grow for happy lovers.

I slip, I slide, I gloom, I glance,
   Among my skimming swallows;
I make the netted sunbeams dance
   Against my sandy shallows.

I murmur under moon and stars
   In brambly wildernesses;
I linger by my shingly bars;
   I loiter round my cresses;

And out again I curve and flow
   To join the brimming river;
For men may come, and men may go,
   But I go on forever.— ALFRED TENNYSON, *The Brook*.

LESSON 121.

Useful suffixes.

In English, suffixes are much more numerous than prefixes.

ed means *did;* as, nod*ded, did* nod.
ing means *continuing;* as, nod*ding, continuing* to nod.

1. Copy carefully. 2. Write from dictation.

1. The world is large when its weary leagues two *loving*
   hearts divide;
   But the world is small when your enemy is loose on
   the other side. — JOHN BOYLE O'REILLY.

2. Sweet are the little brooks that run
   O'er pebbles *glancing* in the sun,
   Singing in *soothing* tones. — THOMAS HOOD.

3. And when they are gone I sit *dreaming*
   Of my childhood too lovely to last. — CHARLES DICKENS.

4. The *rustling* wood, the *dying* breeze,
   The faint low *rippling* of the seas. — FELICIA D. HEMANS.

5. He hath *disgraced* me, and *hindered* me half a
   million; *laughed* at my losses, *mocked* at my
   gains, *scorned* my nation, *thwarted* my bargains,
   cooled my friends, *heated* mine enemies.
   — WILLIAM SHAKESPEARE.

6. See the gold sunshine *patching*,
   And *streaming* and *streaking* across
   The gray-green oaks; and *catching*,
   By its soft brown beard, the moss. — PHILIP JAMES BAILEY.

LESSON 122.

Some words pronounced alike.

1. Copy carefully. 2. Write from dictation. 3. Use the italicized words in sentences of your own.

1. The sea being smooth,
How many shallow bauble boats dare *sail*
Upon her patient breast! — WILLIAM SHAKESPEARE.

2. Of a rank
Too proud for dairy work or *sale* of eggs.
— WILLIAM COWPER.

3. The plentiful moisture encumbered the flower,
And *weighed* down its beautiful head. — WILLIAM COWPER.

4. Should I *wade* no more,
Returning were as tedious as go o'er.
— WILLIAM SHAKESPEARE.

5. Doth it not show vilely in me to desire small *beer?*
— WILLIAM SHAKESPEARE.

6. And e'en the star, that glitters on the *bier*,
Can only say, — Nobility lies here. — WILLIAM COWPER.

7. The sun is couched, the sea*fowl* gone to rest,
And the wild storm hath somewhere found a nest.
— WILLIAM WORDSWORTH.

8. But he that hides a dark soul and *foul* thoughts,
Benighted walks under the midday sun. — JOHN MILTON.

9. It is apparent *foul* play; and 'tis a shame.
WILLIAM SHAKESPEARE.

LESSON 123.

A useful suffix.

ness means *state of being*; as, ill*ness*, *state of being* ill.

1. Copy carefully.   2. Write from dictation.

1. All *wickedness* is *weakness.* — JOHN MILTON.

2. The sunrise wakes the lark to sing,
   The moonrise wakes the nightingale.
   Come *darkness*, moonrise, everything
   That is so silent, sweet, and pale.
   — CHRISTINA G. ROSSETTI.

3. The myrtle dwells there, sending round the *richness* of its breath. — FELICIA D. HEMANS.

4. The *gentleness* of heaven is on the sea.
   — WILLIAM WORDSWORTH.

5. Spurn every vice, each little *meanness* shun.
   — GEORGE GORDON, LORD BYRON.

6. No sound amid night's *stillness*, save that which seemed to be
   The dull and heavy beating of the pulses of the sea.
   — JOHN GREENLEAF WHITTIER.

7. *Stillness* of person and *steadiness* of features are signal marks of good breeding.
   — OLIVER WENDELL HOLMES.

8. It was as if the summer's late
   Atoning for its *sadness*
   Had borrowed every season's charm,
   To end its days in *gladness.* — JOHN GREENLEAF WHITTIER.

LESSON 124.

Some words pronounced alike.

1. Copy carefully. 2. Write from dictation. 3. Use the italicized words in sentences of your own.

1. O, a seraph may *pray* for a sinner,
   But a sinner must *pray* for himself!
   — CHARLES DICKENS.

2. The wild hawk stood with down on his beak
   And stared with his foot on the *prey*.
   — ALFRED TENNYSON.

3. How well I know what I *mean* to do
   When the long autumn evenings come!
   ROBERT BROWNING.

4. His *mien* is lofty, but his gaze
   Too well a wandering soul betrays.
   — FELICIA D. HEMANS.

5. A sense of elegance we rarely find
   The portion of a *mean* or vulgar mind.
   WILLIAM COWPER.

6. The happy *mean* between these two extremes.
   — THOMAS BABINGTON, LORD MACAULAY.

7. Come! let the burial *rite* be read —
   The funeral song be sung. — EDGAR ALLAN POE.

8. Sir, I would rather be *right* than be President.
   HENRY CLAY.

9. And 'tis the sad complaint, and almost true,
   Whate'er we *write*, we bring forth nothing new.
   — WILLIAM COWPER.

LESSON 125.

Useful suffixes.

er, in adjectives, means *more;* as, wis*er*, *more* wise.
est, in adjectives, means *most;* as, wis*est*, *most* wise.

1. Copy carefully.   2. Write from dictation.

1. All that's bright must fade, —
The *brightest* still the *fleetest*. — THOMAS MOORE.

2. Doom'd to that *sorest* task of man alive, —
To make three guineas do the work of five.
ROBERT BURNS.

3. A *lovelier* light on rock and hill, and stream and woodland lay,
And *softer* lapsed on *sunnier* sands the waters of the bay. — JOHN GREENLEAF WHITTIER.

4. 'Tis morn, and nature's *richest* dyes
Are floating o'er Italian skies. — FELICIA D. HEMANS.

5. Spring parts the clouds with *softest* airs,
That she may sun thee. — WILLIAM WORDSWORTH.

6. He was in years just twenty, in his looks much *older*, and in conceit at least two hundred.
— CHARLES DICKENS.

7. I heard the bells, grown *fainter*, far behind me peal and play,
Fainter, fainter, fainter, till they seem'd to die away.
ROBERT BUCHANAN.

8. Flowers are the *sweetest* things God ever made, and forgot to put a soul into. — HENRY WARD BEECHER.

LESSON 126.

Some words pronounced alike.

1. Copy carefully.   2. Write from dictation.   3. Use the italicized words in sentences of your own.

1. *Seam* and gusset and band,
   Band and gusset and *seam*, —
   Till the heart is sick and the brain benumbed,
   As well as the weary hand. — THOMAS HOOD.

2. The Earth and Ocean *seem* to sleep.
   PERCY BYSSHE SHELLEY.

3. He shows, on holidays, a sacred pin
   That touch'd the *ruff* that touch'd Queen Bess's chin.
   — EDWARD YOUNG.

4. *Rough* winds do shake the darling buds of May.
   — WILLIAM SHAKESPEARE.

5. Why does the sea *moan* evermore?
   — CHRISTINA G. ROSSETTI.

6. And oft, when the summer sun shone hot
   On the new-*mown* hay in the meadow lot,
   And she heard the little spring brook fall
   Over the roadside, through the wall.
   — JOHN GREENLEAF WHITTIER.

7. And all that she has made of that
   Is one poor pound of *tow*. — ROBERT BURNS.

8. Come and trip it as you go,
   On the light fantastic *toe*. — JOHN MILTON.

JOHN GREENLEAF WHITTIER

1807 ⚜ 1892

LESSON 127.

A useful suffix.

er, in nouns, means *one who* or *that which;* as, teach*er*, *one who* teaches; heat*er*, *that which* heats.

  1. Copy carefully.   2. Write from dictation.

1. In the elder days of Art
   Builders wrought with greatest care
   Each minute and unseen part;
   For the Gods see everywhere.
   — HENRY WADSWORTH LONGFELLOW.

2. Sweet shadows of twilight! how calm they repose,
   While the dewdrops fall soft in the breast of the rose!
   How blest to the *toiler* his hour of release
   When the vesper is heard with its whisper of peace.
   — OLIVER WENDELL HOLMES.

3. Our friends the *reviewers*, those *clippers* and *hewers*.
   ROBERT BURNS.

4. How ill white hairs become a fool and *jester!*
   — WILLIAM SHAKESPEARE.

5. And hark! how blithe the throstle sings!
   He, too, is no mean *preacher:*
   Come forth into the light of things,
   Let Nature be your *teacher.* — WILLIAM WORDSWORTH.

6. And He from the mighty *doubter*
   The great *believer* makes. — RICHARD WATSON GILDER.

7. That old bald *cheater*, Time. — BEN JONSON.

LESSON 128.

Some words pronounced alike.

1. Copy carefully.   2. Write from dictation.   3. Use the italicized words in sentences of your own.

1. His *sole* opinion, whatsoe'er befall,
   Centering at last in having none at all.
   — WILLIAM COWPER.

2. From the crown of his head to the *sole* of his foot, he is all mirth. — WILLIAM SHAKESPEARE.

3. Oh, God! it is a fearful thing
   To see the human *soul* take wing!
   — GEORGE GORDON, LORD BYRON.

4. And, jealous of the listening air,
   They *steal* their way from stair to stair.
   — SAMUEL TAYLOR COLERIDGE.

5. Years following years *steal* something ev'ry day;
   At last they *steal* us from ourselves away.
   — ALEXANDER POPE.

6. Whose golden touch could soften *steel* and stones,
   Make tigers tame. — WILLIAM SHAKESPEARE.

7. I thought it most prudent to defer the *drafts* till advice was received of the progress of the loan.
   ALEXANDER HAMILTON.

8. The merrier up its roaring *draught*
   The great throat of the chimney laughed.
   — JOHN GREENLEAF WHITTIER.

9. O, for a *draught* of vintage! that hath been
   Cool'd a long age in the deep-delved earth.
   — JOHN KEATS.

LESSON 129.

A useful suffix.

en, in adjectives, means *made of;* in verbs, *to make;* as, wood*en*, *made of* wood; short*en*, *to make* short.

1. Copy carefully.   2. Write from dictation.

1. Toned the *golden* clouds, sun-painted,
   Till they paled, and paled, and fainted
   From the face of heaven away. — EDMUND WALLER.

2. The balmy gales awake the flowers,
   And wave thy *flaxen* hair. — ROBERT BURNS.

3. So joys, remembered, without wish or will,
   Sharpen the keenest edge of present ill.
   — WILLIAM WORDSWORTH.

4. Oft the cloud which wraps the present hour
   Serves but to *brighten* all our future days.
   — JOHN BROWN.

5. There's a dance of leaves in that *aspen* bower,
   There's a titter of winds in that *beechen* tree,
   There's a smile on the fruit, and a smile on the flower,
   And a laugh from the brook that runs to the sea.
   — WILLIAM CULLEN BRYANT.

6. There now the sun had sunk; but lines of gold
   Hung on the *ashen* clouds. — PERCY BYSSHE SHELLEY.

7. When life was like a story, holding neither sob nor sigh,
   In the *golden olden* glory of the days gone by.
   — JAMES WHITCOMB RILEY.

LESSON 130.

Some words pronounced alike.

1. Copy carefully.   2. Write from dictation.   3. Use the italicized words in sentences of your own.

1. If it were *done* when 'tis *done*, then 'twere well
   It were *done* quickly. — WILLIAM SHAKESPEARE.

2. Amid the gliding waves and shadows *dun*.
   PERCY BYSSHE SHELLEY.

3. Did Adam have *duns* and slip down a back-lane?
   JAMES RUSSELL LOWELL.

4. In his *fore* leg there was a splinter of wood, and he was miserably lame. — DOCTOR JOHN BROWN.

5. If I could bid the fifth welcome with so good a heart as I can the other *four* farewell, I should be glad. — WILLIAM SHAKESPEARE.

6. When chill November's surly blast
   Made fields and forests *bare*. — ROBERT BURNS.

7. I never knew any man in my life who could not *bear* another's misfortunes perfectly like a Christian. — ALEXANDER POPE.

8.   Of all the trees
   In paradise that *bear* delicious fruit. — JOHN MILTON.

9. In the night, imagining some fear,
   How easy is a bush supposed a *bear*.
   — WILLIAM SHAKESPEARE.

LESSON 131.

A useful suffix.

ish means *like* or *somewhat;* as, child*ish, like* a child; sweet*ish, somewhat* sweet.

1. Copy carefully. 2. Write from dictation.

1. He will not blush, that has a father's heart,
   To take in *childish* plays a *childish* part.
   — WILLIAM COWPER.

2. A *knavish* speech sleeps in a *foolish* ear.
   — WILLIAM SHAKESPEARE.

3. Think you 'twill matter a few score years hence what our *foolish* honors to-day are?
   — WILLIAM MAKEPEACE THACKERAY.

4. We'll talk of sunshine and of song;
   And summer days when we were young;
   Sweet *childish* days, that were as long
   As twenty days are now. — WILLIAM WORDSWORTH.

5. Four and twenty times the pilot's glass
   Hath told the *thievish* minutes how they pass.
   — WILLIAM SHAKESPEARE.

6. Her eye is hazel and bright; and now and then she turns it on me with a look of *girlish* curiosity.
   DONALD G. MITCHELL.

7. True power was never born of *brutish* strength.
   JAMES RUSSELL LOWELL.

8. On inquiry, found that "the boys" were certain *baldish* and *grayish* old gentlemen that one sees or hears of in various important stations of society. — OLIVER WENDELL HOLMES.

LESSON 132.

Some words pronounced alike.

1. Copy carefully. 2. Write from dictation. 3. Use the italicized words in sentences of your own.

1. And let your silver chime
   Move in melodious time,
   And let the *bass* of Heaven's deep organ blow.
   — JOHN MILTON.

2. The one *base* thing in the universe — to receive favors and to render none. — RALPH WALDO EMERSON.

3. Around its *base* the bare rocks stood. — THOMAS MOORE.

4. He wandered far; much did he see of men,
   Their manners, *their* enjoyments, and pursuits.
   — WILLIAM WORDSWORTH.

5. And none speaks false, when *there* is none to hear.
   — JAMES BEATTIE.

6. So nigh to the great warm heart of God,
   You almost seem to feel it *beat*. — JAMES RUSSELL LOWELL.

7. I found by experiment that I could make a very good molasses either of pumpkins or *beets*.
   — HENRY DAVID THOREAU.

8. The Lotos blooms below the barren peak;
   The Lotos blooms by every winding *creek*.
   — ALFRED TENNYSON.

9. Not more distinct from harmony divine
   The constant *creaking* of a country sign.
   — WILLIAM COWPER.

LESSON 133.

A useful suffix.

ly means *like* or *in a manner;* as, man*ly*, *like* a man; brave*ly*, *in a* brave *manner.*

1. Copy carefully.   2. Write from dictation.

1. I heard the thunder *hoarsely* laugh;
Mighty fleets were strewn like chaff.
— PERCY BYSSHE SHELLEY.

2. The winds with wonder whist
Smoothly the waters kist
Whisp'ring new joys to the wild ocean. — JOHN MILTON.

3. Heard a carol, mournful, holy,
Chanted *loudly*, chanted *lowly*. — ALFRED TENNYSON.

4. He felt the soft breeze at its frolicsome play;
He smelled the sweet odor of *newly* mown hay.
— THOMAS DUNN ENGLISH.

5. The butterfly, all green and gold,
To me hath often flown,
Here in my blossoms to behold
Wings *lovely* as his own. — WILLIAM WORDSWORTH.

6. Blue, *darkly, deeply, beautifully* blue. — ROBERT SOUTHEY.

7. We must all hang together or *assuredly* we shall all hang *separately.* — BENJAMIN FRANKLIN.

8. Give me the *lonely* valley,
The dewy eve, and rising moon. — ROBERT BURNS.

LESSON 134.

Some words pronounced alike.

1. Copy carefully. 2. Write from dictation. 3. Use the italicized words in sentences of your own.

1. Rare are solitary woes;
They love a train, they tread each other's *heel*.
— EDWARD YOUNG.

2. How poor are they that have not patience!
What wound did ever *heal* but by degrees?
— WILLIAM SHAKESPEARE.

3. It is as great a *bore* as to hear a poet read his own verses. — NATHANIEL HAWTHORNE.

4. The music in my heart I *bore*,
Long after it was heard no more.
— WILLIAM WORDSWORTH.

5. Have I not heard the sea puff'd up with winds
Rage like an angry *boar?* — WILLIAM SHAKESPEARE.

6. Comes at the last and with a little pin
Bores through his castle wall. — WILLIAM SHAKESPEARE.

7. Don't you know how hard it is for some people to get out of a room after their visit is really over? They want to be off, and you want to have them off, *but* they don't know how to manage it. — OLIVER WENDELL HOLMES.

8. The very *butt* of Slander, and the blot
For every dart that Malice ever shot. — WILLIAM COWPER.

OLIVER WENDELL HOLMES

1809 ⁕ 1894

LESSON 135.

A useful suffix.

y means *having* or *full of;* as, lucky, *having* luck; smoky, *full of* smoke.

1. Copy carefully. 2. Write from dictation.

1. Behold, within the *leafy* shade,
 Those bright blue eggs together laid!
 — WILLIAM WORDSWORTH.

2. The sun looks o'er, with *hazy* eye,
 The *snowy* mountain-tops which lie
 Piled coldly up against the sky.
 — JOHN GREENLEAF WHITTIER.

3. The bliss which wing'd those *rosy* hours
 Was such as pleasure seldom showers
 On mortals here below. — GEORGE GORDON, LORD BYRON.

4. Met by the rainbow's form divine
 Issuing from her *cloudy* shrine. — WILLIAM WORDSWORTH.

5. Where earth and sky in *dreamy* distance meet.
 JAMES A. GARFIELD.

6. A *drowsy, dreamy* influence seems to hang over the land, and to pervade the very atmosphere.
 WASHINGTON IRVING.

7. A *heavy* heart bears not a nimble tongue.
 — WILLIAM SHAKESPEARE.

8. The stone hut was made a soft nest for her, lined with *downy* patience. — GEORGE ELIOT.

LESSON 136.

Some words pronounced alike.

1. Copy carefully. 2. Write from dictation. 3. Use the italicized words in sentences of your own.

1. Was smooth and even as an ivory *ball*.
—WILLIAM COWPER.

2. In various talk the instructive hours they past,
Who gave the *ball*, or paid the visit last.
ALEXANDER POPE.

3.   Casting pearl to hogs;
That *bawl* for freedom in their senseless mood.
JOHN MILTON.

4. On greasy *steaks* from chop-house did regale.
—MARCUS V. MARTIAL.

5. But they that fight for freedom undertake
The noblest cause mankind can have at *stake*.
— WILLIAM COWPER.

6. To one fixed *stake* my spirit clings;
I know that God is good!—JOHN GREENLEAF WHITTIER.

7. So when the sun in bed,
Curtain'd with cloudy red,
Pillows his chin upon an orient *wave*.—JOHN MILTON.

8. Aspen leaves that *wave* without a wind.
JOHN LEYDEN.

9. I have so great a love for you that I can *waive* opportunities of gain to help you.
—SIR RICHARD STEELE.

LESSON 137.

A useful suffix.

less means *without;* as, home*less, without* a home.

1. Copy carefully. 2. Write from dictation.

1. The sacred river ran,
   Through caverns *measureless* to man,
   Down to a *sunless* sea. — SAMUEL TAYLOR COLERIDGE.

2. The wild wind slumbers in its cave,
   And heaven is *cloudless* — earth is still!
   — FELICIA D. HEMANS.

3.   Silence, and a *stirless* breath
   Which neither was of life nor death;
   A sea of stagnant idleness,
   Blind, *boundless*, mute, and *motionless!*
   — GEORGE GORDON, LORD BYRON.

4. The *deathless* stars are bright above.
   — PERCY BYSSHE SHELLEY.

5.   The everlasting hills
   Changeless watch the *changeless* heavens.
   — CHARLES KINGSLEY.

6. With *noiseless* step sweet memory comes.
   — JAMES A. GARFIELD.

7. And all the incense in the air springs from the
      speechless sod,
   Which has no other offering or way to worship God.
   CHARLES MONROE DICKINSON.

8. Drown'd in yonder living blue
   The lark becomes a *sightless* song. — ALFRED TENNYSON.

LESSON 138.

Some words pronounced alike.

1. Copy carefully. 2. Write from dictation. 3. Use the italicized words in sentences of your own.

1. Now do I feel
    Of what *coarse* metal ye are moulded, envy!
    — WILLIAM SHAKESPEARE.

2. How fine has the day been! How bright was the sun,
    How lovely and joyful the *course* that he run!
    — ISAAC WATTS.

3. And pacing through the forest,
    He *chews* the food of sweet and bitter fancy.
    WILLIAM SHAKESPEARE.

4. *Choose* an author as you *choose* a friend.
    — WENTWORTH DILLON.

5. The lark sung loud the music at his heart,
    And bore in Nature's *choir* the merriest part.
    CHARLES TENNYSON TURNER.

6. With an ounce of poison in one pocket
    And a *quire* of bad verses in the other.
    THOMAS BABINGTON, LORD MACAULAY.

7. Too late I *stayed*, — forgive the crime;
    Unheeded flew the hours,
    How noiseless falls the foot of time
    That only treads on flowers! — WILLIAM R. SPENCER.

8. O'erlaid with black, *staid* wisdom's hue. — JOHN MILTON.

LESSON 139.

A useful suffix.

ous means *full of;* as, joy*ous, full of* joy.

  1. Copy carefully.   2. Write from dictation.

1. The airs and streams renew their *joyous* tones.
   — PERCY BYSSHE SHELLEY.

2. And early, ere the *odorous* breath of morn
   Awakes the slumbering leaves. — JOHN MILTON.

3. The *envious* will die, but envy never. — MOLIÈRE.

4. I stood upon the hills, when heaven's wide arch
   Was *glorious* with the sun's returning march.
   — HENRY WADSWORTH LONGFELLOW.

5. Some temptations come to the *industrious*, but all temptations attack the idle. — CHARLES H. SPURGEON.

6. The wilderness has a *mysterious* tongue.
   — PERCY BYSSHE SHELLEY.

7. Nothing is so *dangerous* as an ignorant friend; a wise enemy is worth more. — LA FONTAINE.

8. I hear the bell's *melodious* din,
   I hear the organ peal within.
   — HENRY WADSWORTH LONGFELLOW.

9. Whose *humorous* vein, strong sense, and simple style,
   May teach the gayest, make the gravest smile.
   — WILLIAM COWPER.

LESSON 140.

Some words pronounced alike.

1. Copy carefully. 2. Write from dictation. 3. Use the italicized words in sentences of your own.

1. And if thou want'st a *cord*, the smallest thread
   That ever spider twisted
   Will serve to strangle thee. — WILLIAM SHAKESPEARE.

2. *Chords* that vibrate sweetest pleasure,
   Thrill the deepest notes of woe. — ROBERT BURNS.

3.   Pity and need
   Make all flesh kin. There is no *caste* in blood.
                            — EDWIN ARNOLD.

4. The daisy, by the shadow that it *casts*,
   Protects the lingering dewdrop from the sun.
                            — WILLIAM WORDSWORTH.

5. As *chaste* as is the bud ere it be blown.
                            — WILLIAM SHAKESPEARE.

6. Aurora had but newly *chased* the night,
   And purpled o'er the sky with blushing light.
                            JOHN DRYDEN.

7. And the *maize*-field grew and ripened,
   Till it stood in all the splendor
   Of its garments green and yellow.
                    — HENRY WADSWORTH LONGFELLOW.

8. Through the verdant *maze*
   Of sweetbrier hedges I pursue my walk.
                            — JAMES THOMSON.

LESSON 141.

A useful suffix.

able means *able to be, fit to be,* or *causing;* as, eat*able, fit to be* eaten; bear*able, able to be* borne.

1. Copy carefully.   2. Write from dictation.

1. To be loved, be *lovable.* — OVID.

2. A most *notable* coward, an infinite and endless liar.
— WILLIAM SHAKESPEARE.

3. Animals are such *agreeable* friends — they ask no questions, they pass no criticisms. — GEORGE ELIOT.

4. There is no good arguing with the *inevitable.* The only argument *available* with an east wind is to put on your overcoat. — JAMES RUSSELL LOWELL.

5.   And *variable* as the shade
By the light quivering aspen made. — SIR WALTER SCOTT.

6. The *illimitable,* silent, never-resting thing called Time, rolling, rushing on, swift, silent.
THOMAS CARLYLE.

7. Think'st thou it *honorable* for a noble man
Still to remember wrongs? — WILLIAM SHAKESPEARE.

8. His coat-sleeves being a great deal too long, and his trousers a great deal too short, he appeared ill at ease in his clothes, as if he were in a perpetual state of astonishment at finding himself so *respectable.* — CHARLES DICKENS.

LESSON 142.

Some words pronounced alike.

1. Copy carefully.   2. Write from dictation.   3. Use the italicized words in sentences of your own.

1. The little waves, with their soft, white hands,
   Efface the footprints in the sands,
   And the *tide* rises, the *tide* falls.
   — HENRY WADSWORTH LONGFELLOW.

2. Thus going the rounds of the neighborhood, with all his worldly effects *tied* up in a cotton handkerchief. — WASHINGTON IRVING.

3. The lav'rock shuns the palace gay,
   And o'er the cottage sings;
   For nature smiles as sweet, I *ween*,
   To shepherds as to kings. — ROBERT BURNS.

4. By fire and storm, Heaven tries the Christian's worth,
   And joy departs, to *wean* us from the earth.
   — FELICIA D. HEMANS.

5. As bees fly home with loads of treasure,
   The minutes wing'd their *way* with pleasure.
   — ROBERT BURNS.

6. How many thousand of my poorest subjects
   Are at this hour asleep! O sleep, O gentle sleep,
   Nature's soft nurse, how have I frighted thee,
   That thou no more wilt *weigh* my eyelids down
   And steep my senses in forgetfulness?
   — WILLIAM SHAKESPEARE.

LESSON 143.

A useful suffix.

ful means *full of;* as, joy*ful, full of* joy.

1. Copy carefully. 2. Write from dictation.

1. These are certain signs to know,
    Faithful friend from flattering foe.
    — WILLIAM SHAKESPEARE.

2. A voice of sorrow swells in every gale,
    Each wave low rippling tells a *mournful* tale.
    — FELICIA D. HEMANS.

3. To be seventy years young is sometimes far more *cheerful* and *hopeful* than to be forty years old.
    — OLIVER WENDELL HOLMES.

4. Such sights as *youthful* poets dream
    On summer eves by haunted stream. — JOHN MILTON.

5. More *helpful* than all wisdom is one draught of simple pity that will not forsake us.
    — GEORGE ELIOT.

6. From room to room I hear the *wakeful* clocks
    Challenge the passing hour.
    — HENRY WADSWORTH LONGFELLOW.

7. Applause from old friends and neighbors is the most *grateful* that ever reaches human ears.
    — JAMES G. BLAINE.

8. Nothing is more *useful* than silence. — MENANDER.

9. We are apt to shut our eyes against a *painful* truth.
    — PATRICK HENRY.

LESSON 144.

Some words pronounced alike.

1. Copy carefully.   2. Write from dictation.   3. Use the italicized words in sentences of your own.

1. Without a sign his *sword* the brave man draws,
   And asks no omen but his country's cause. — HOMER.

2.   The fondest hope
   That ever *soared* on fancy's wildest wing!
                        — PERCY BYSSHE SHELLEY.

3. It is the *hour* when from the boughs
   The nightingale's high note is heard:
   It is the *hour* when lovers' vows
   Seem sweet in every whisper'd word.
                   GEORGE GORDON, LORD BYRON.

4. The doorstep to the temple of wisdom is a knowledge of *our* own ignorance. — CHARLES H. SPURGEON.

5.   To hang
   Quite out of fashion, like a rusty *mail*
   In monumental mockery. — WILLIAM SHAKESPEARE.

6. Every creature, female as the *male*,
   Stands single in responsible act and thought.
                     ELIZABETH BARRETT BROWNING.

7. As from the road with sudden sweep
   The *Mail* drove up the little steep,
   And stopped beside the tavern door.
                   HENRY WADSWORTH LONGFELLOW.

LESSON 145.

A useful prefix.

un means *not* or *the opposite act;* as, *un*safe, *not* safe; *un*tie, *the opposite of* tie, to loose.

1. Copy carefully.   2. Write from dictation.

1.   Nature too *unkind*,
That made no medicine for a troubled mind.
FRANCIS BEAUMONT AND JOHN FLETCHER.

2. Why should we yet our sail *unfurl?*
There is not a breath the blue wave to curl.
THOMAS MOORE.

3. Far up the blue sky, a fair rainbow *unrolled*
Its soft-tinted pinions of purple and gold.
— AMELIA B. WELBY.

4. And the flower, as it listens, *unconsciously* dips,
Till the rising wave glistens and kisses its lips.
JOHN FRANCIS WALLER.

5. And thanks *untraced* to lips *unknown*
Shall greet us like the odors blown
From *unseen* meadows newly mown.
JOHN GREENLEAF WHITTIER.

6. Spring *unlocks* the flowers to paint the laughing soil.
— REGINALD HEBER.

7. The earth *unfolds* her loveliness to the just and to the *unjust.* — GAIL HAMILTON.

8. It is better to be *unborn* than *untaught;* for ignorance is the root of misfortune. — PLATO.

LESSON 146.

Some words pronounced alike.

1. Copy carefully. 2. Write from dictation. 3. Use the italicized words in sentences of your own.

1. Some glory in their *birth*, some in their skill,
   Some in their wealth. — WILLIAM SHAKESPEARE.

2. I waked every morning with the belief that some one was tipping up my *berth*.
   — RALPH WALDO EMERSON.

3. It is a beauteous Evening, calm and free;
   The holy time is quiet as a *Nun*
   Breathless with adoration; the broad sun
   Is sinking down in its tranquillity;
   The gentleness of heaven is on the Sea.
   WILLIAM WORDSWORTH.

4. Ah, thought I, thou mourn'st in vain!
   None takes pity on thy pain:
   Even so, poor bird, like thee,
   None alive will pity me. — WILLIAM SHAKESPEARE.

5. Society is now one polish'd *horde*,
   Form'd of two mighty tribes, the Bores and Bored.
   GEORGE GORDON, LORD BYRON.

6. Heap high the farmer's wintry *hoard*!
   Heap high the golden corn!
   No richer gift has Autumn poured
   From out her lavish horn! — JOHN GREENLEAF WHITTIER.

LESSON 147.

A useful prefix.

mis means *wrong* or *wrongly;* as, *mis*conduct, *wrong* conduct; *mis*judge, to judge *wrongly*.

1. Copy carefully.   2. Write from dictation.

1. King's *misdeeds* cannot be hid in clay.
   WILLIAM SHAKESPEARE.

2. History, which is, indeed, little more than the register of the crimes, follies, and *misfortunes* of mankind.
   — EDWARD GIBBON.

3. I saw an uneasy change in Mr. Micawber, which sat lightly on him, as if his new duties were a *misfit*. — CHARLES DICKENS.

4. Men deal with life as children with their play,
   Who first *misuse*, then cast their toys away.
   — WILLIAM COWPER.

5.   Sleep hath its own world,
   A boundary between the things *misnamed*
   Death and existence. — GEORGE GORDON, LORD BYRON.

6. And who would murmur and *misdoubt*,
   When God's great sunrise finds him out?
   — ELIZABETH BARRETT BROWNING.

7. It is not safe for any man to ride so near the edge of disaster that if he makes one *misstep* it will plunge him into ruin. — HENRY WARD BEECHER.

Caution. Do not double the *s* in *mis*, and do not drop the *s* when the root word begins with *s*.

LESSON 148.

Some words pronounced alike.

1. Copy carefully. 2. Write from dictation. 3. Use the italicized words in sentences of your own.

1.   Mountains rear
To heaven their bald and blacken'd cliffs, and bow
Their tall heads to the *plain*. — GEORGE D. PRENTICE.

2. There are some people that never see anything, if it is as *plain* as a hole in a grindstone, until it is pointed out to them. — OLIVER WENDELL HOLMES.

3. The slanting sunbeams shone through the transparent shavings that flew before the sturdy *plane*. — GEORGE ELIOT.

4. Oh, for a lever that would lift
Thought to a higher *plane!* — ALICE CARY.

5. The sounding *aisles* of the dim woods rang
To the anthem of the free. — FELICIA D. HEMANS.

6. And then there was a little *isle*,
Which in my very face did smile,
The only one in view. — GEORGE GORDON, LORD BYRON.

7. For her *I'll* dare the billows' roar,
For her *I'll* trace a distant shore. — ROBERT BURNS.

LESSON 149.
A useful prefix.

re means *back* or *again;* as, *re*call, to call *back;* *re*join, to join *again.*

   1. Copy carefully.   2. Write from dictation.

1.   The clouds of eve
Reflect unmoved the lingering beam of day.
PERCY BYSSHE SHELLEY.

2. He is great who is what he is from Nature, and who never *reminds* us of others.
— RALPH WALDO EMERSON.

3. Memory watches o'er the sad *review*
Of joys that faded like the morning dew.
THOMAS CAMPBELL.

4. The sprightly morn her course *renewed*
And evening gray again ensued. — WILLIAM COWPER.

5. And listen many a grateful bird
Return you tuneful thanks. — ROBERT BURNS.

6.   The fields *revive*,
The birds their notes *renew*, and bleating herds
Attest their joy. — JOHN MILTON.

7. In order to profit by what we have learned, we must think; that is, *reflect*. He only thinks who *reflects*. — SAMUEL TAYLOR COLERIDGE.

8. I love to rove o'er History's page,
Recall the hero and the sage. — FELICIA D. HEMANS.

LESSON 150.

Some words pronounced alike.

1. Copy carefully. 2. Write from dictation. 3. Use the italicized words in sentences of your own.

1. The full notes closer grow;
   Hark what a torrent gush!
   They *pour*, they overflow —
   Sing on, sing on, O thrush! — AUSTIN DOBSON.

2. Gathering virtue in at every *pore*.
   — JAMES RUSSELL LOWELL.

3. There at the foot of yonder nodding beech,
   That wreathes its old fantastic roots so high,
   His listless length at noontide would he stretch,
   And *pore* upon the brook that babbles by.
   — THOMAS GRAY.

4. Gracious as sunshine, sweet as dew
   Shut in a lily's golden *core*. — MARGARET J. PRESTON.

5. Bright Phœbus ne'er witnessed so joyous a *corps*.
   — ROBERT BURNS.

6. Heaven from all creatures hides the book of *fate*.
   ALEXANDER POPE.

7. They remembered Garrick, the prime mover of the *fête*. — WASHINGTON IRVING.

8. What will this sister of mine do with *rice*?
   WILLIAM SHAKESPEARE.

9. The approach to the house was by a gentle *rise* and through an avenue of noble trees. — MARK LEMON.

LESSON 151.

A useful prefix.

dis often means *not* or the *opposite act;* as, dishonest, *not* honest; disagree, the *opposite* of agree, to differ.

1. Copy carefully.   2. Write from dictation.

1. Bid the *dishonest* man mend himself; if he mend he is no longer *dishonest.* — WILLIAM SHAKESPEARE.

2. It is the *disease* of not listening that I am troubled with. — WILLIAM SHAKESPEARE.

3. But where will fierce contention end,
   If flowers can *disagree?* — WILLIAM COWPER.

4. What most he should *dislike* seems pleasant to him.
   — WILLIAM SHAKESPEARE.

5. He *distrusted* her affection; and what loneliness is more lonely than *distrust?* — GEORGE ELIOT.

6. The only dish which excited our appetites and *disappointed* our stomachs in almost equal proportion. — CHARLES LAMB.

7. Love, anger, and despair,
   The phantoms of *disordered* sense.
   JOHN GREENLEAF WHITTIER.

8. But my five wits nor my five senses can
   Dissuade one foolish heart from serving thee.
   WILLIAM SHAKESPEARE.

Caution. Do not double the *s* in *dis,* and do not drop the *s* when the root word begins with *s*.

LESSON 152.

Some words pronounced alike.

1. Copy carefully. 2. Write from dictation. 3. Use the italicized words in sentences of your own.

1. A finch, whose tongue knew no control,
   With golden wing and satin *poll*. — WILLIAM COWPER.

2. Some fickle creatures boast a soul
   True as a needle to the *pole*. — WILLIAM COWPER.

3. Dancing round a *pole* dressed up with wreaths
   On May-day. — PERCY BYSSHE SHELLEY.

4. Where to the sky the *rude* sea rarely smiles.
   — PERCY BYSSHE SHELLEY.

5. Covering many a *rood* of ground,
   Lay the timber piled around.
   HENRY WADSWORTH LONGFELLOW.

6.   The wind of May
   Is *sweet* with breath of orchards.
   — WILLIAM CULLEN BRYANT.

7.   Prepare yourself, my Lord.
   Our *suite* will join yours in the court below.
   PERCY BYSSHE SHELLEY.

8. Took one of the candles that stood upon the king's table and lighted his Majesty through a *suite* of rooms. — JAMES BOSWELL.

9.   The bee
   Sits on the bloom, extracting liquid *sweet*.
   — JOHN MILTON.

LESSON 153.

1. Copy carefully. 2. Write from dictation, or from memory.

I visited various parts of my own country; and on no country have the charms of nature been more prodigally lavished. Her mighty lakes, like oceans of liquid silver; her mountains, with their bright aerial tints; her valleys, teeming with wild fertility; her tremendous cataracts, thundering in their solitudes; her boundless plains, waving with spontaneous verdure; her broad, deep rivers, rolling in solemn silence to the ocean; her trackless forests, where vegetation puts forth all its magnificence; her skies, kindling with the magic of summer clouds and glorious sunshine: — no, never need an American look beyond his own country for the sublime and beautiful of natural scenery.

But Europe held forth all the charms of storied and poetical association. There were to be seen the masterpieces of art, the refinements of highly cultivated society, the quaint peculiarities of ancient and local custom. My native country was full of youthful promise; Europe was rich in the accumulated treasures of age. Her very ruins told the history of times gone by, and every mouldering stone was a chronicle. I longed to wander over the scenes of renowned achievement, — to tread, as it were, in the footsteps of antiquity; to loiter about the ruined castle; to meditate on the falling tower, — to escape, in short, from the commonplace realities of the present, and lose myself among the shadowy grandeurs of the past. — WASHINGTON IRVING.

LESSON 154.

Some words pronounced alike.

1. Copy carefully. 2. Write from dictation. 3. Use the italicized words in sentences of your own.

1. The merry plowboy cheers his *team*. — ROBERT BURNS.

2. Now *teem* with countless rills and shady woods,
Cornfields and pastures and white cottages.
— PERCY BYSSHE SHELLEY.

3. But for their sake my heart doth ache,
With many a bitter *throe*. — ROBERT BURNS.

4. Up the rude crags, whose giant masses *throw*
Eternal shadows o'er the glen below.
— FELICIA D. HEMANS.

5. Not many sounds in life exceed in interest a knock at the door. It "gives a very echo to the *throne* where hope is seated." — CHARLES LAMB.

6. The shiver of dancing leaves is *thrown*
About its echoing chambers wide. — ALFRED TENNYSON.

7. And faint, from farther distance *borne*,
Were heard the clanging hoof and horn.
— SIR WALTER SCOTT.

8.   Take your imagination,
From *bourn* to *bourn*, region to region.
— WILLIAM SHAKESPEARE.

9. In his high place he had so *borne* himself that all had feared him, that most had loved him.
THOMAS BABINGTON, LORD MACAULAY.

ALFRED

1809

LESSON 155.

Some words pronounced alike.

1. Copy carefully.   2. Write from dictation.   3. Use the italicized words in sentences of your own.

1. The ceaseless rain is falling fast,
   And yonder gilded *vane*,
   Immovable for three days past,
   Points to the misty main.
   — HENRY WADSWORTH LONGFELLOW.

2. Pass, therefore, not to-day in *vain*,
   For it will never come again. — OMAR KHAYYAM.

3. Consult Life's silent clock, thy bounding *vein*;
   Seems it to say, — "Life here has long to reign"?
   — WILLIAM COWPER.

4. Soothed with the sound, the king grew *vain*;
   Fought all his battles o'er again. — JOHN DRYDEN.

5. And which is the best I leave to be *guessed*.
   — PERCY BYSSHE SHELLEY.

6. Wealth without virtue is a dangerous *guest*;
   Who holds them mingled is supremely blest. — SAPPHO.

7. But the Sensitive Plant could give small fruit
   Of the love which it felt from the leaf to the *root*.
   — PERCY BYSSHE SHELLEY.

8. We alighted at some place, which is as little within my distinct remembrance as the *route* by which we reached it. — THOMAS DE QUINCEY.

LESSON 156.

Some words pronounced alike.

1. Copy carefully. 2. Write from dictation. 3. Use the italicized words in sentences of your own.

1. And above his head he *sees*
   The clear moon, the glory of the heavens.
   —WILLIAM WORDSWORTH.

2. But pleasures are like poppies spread,
   You *seize* the flow'r, its bloom is shed. —ROBERT BURNS.

3. All habits gather by unseen degrees,
   As brooks make rivers, rivers run to *seas*.
   —JOHN DRYDEN.

4. Of this alone even God is deprived, the power of making things that are past never to have *been*.
   —AGATHON.

5. For they love to hear on the roof, the rain,
   And to count the *bins*, again and again,
   Heaped with their treasures of golden grain.
   PHŒBE CARY.

6.   The innocent sleep,
   Sleep that knits up the ravell'd sleeve of care,
   The death of each day's life, *sore* labor's bath,
   Balm of hurt minds. —WILLIAM SHAKESPEARE.

7. 'Tis but a base ignoble mind
   That mounts no higher than a bird can *soar*.
   —WILLIAM SHAKESPEARE.

LESSON 157.

Some words pronounced alike.

1. Copy carefully. 2. Write from dictation. 3. Use the italicized words in sentences of your own.

1. Sweets for a hundred flowery springs
   To *load* the May-wind's restless wings.
   — WILLIAM CULLEN BRYANT.

2. That *load* becomes light which is cheerfully borne.
   — OVID.

3. Your eyes are *lode*-stars. — WILLIAM SHAKESPEARE.

4.   *Slight* as some cloud
   That catches but the palest tinge of day.
   — PERCY BYSSHE SHELLEY.

5. The beauteous pink I would not *slight*.
   — JOHANN W. GOETHE.

6. You see he (a trout) lies still, and the *sleight* is to land him. — ISAAC WALTON.

7.   Such guiltless pride,
   As murderers cannot *feign*. — PERCY BYSSHE SHELLEY.

8. *Fain* would I pause to dwell upon the world of charms that burst upon the enraptured gaze of my hero. — WASHINGTON IRVING.

9. Thou hast fair forms that move
    With queenly tread;
   Thou hast proud *fanes* above
    Thy mighty dead. — FELICIA D. HEMANS.

LESSON 158.

Some words pronounced alike.

1. Copy carefully. 2. Write from dictation. 3. Use the italicized words in sentences of your own.

1. *Freeze, freeze,* thou bitter sky,
   That dost not bite so nigh
   As benefits forgot. — WILLIAM SHAKESPEARE.

2. Here vanity assumes her pert grimace,
   And trims her robes of *frieze* with copper lace.
   — OLIVER GOLDSMITH.

3. Swallows have nearly choked up every chimney with their nests; martins build in every *frieze* and cornice; and crows flutter about the towers.
   — WASHINGTON IRVING.

4. The construction of a fable seems by no means the *forte* of our modern poetical writers.
   — LORD FRANCIS JEFFREY.

5. Hold the *Fort!* I am coming.
   — WILLIAM TECUMSEH SHERMAN.

6. I love this gray old church, the low, long *nave,*
   The ivied chancel and the slender spire.
   JEAN INGELOW.

7. An honest man, sir, is able to speak for himself,
   When a *knave* is not. — WILLIAM SHAKESPEARE.

8. Break all the spokes and fellies from her wheel,
   And bowl the round *nave* down the hill.
   — WILLIAM SHAKESPEARE.

LESSON 159.

Some words pronounced alike.

1. Copy carefully. 2. Write from dictation. 3. Use the italicized words in sentences of your own.

1. At last men came to set me free,
   I ask'd not why, and *reck'd* not where.
   — GEORGE GORDON, LORD BYRON.

2. Like golden ripples hasting to the land
   To *wreck* their freight of sunshine on the strand.
   —JAMES RUSSELL LOWELL.

3. The manly part is to do with *might* and main what you can do. — RALPH WALDO EMERSON.

4. For of all sad words of tongue or pen,
   The saddest are these: "It *might* have been!"
   —JOHN GREENLEAF WHITTIER.

5. For life is so high a perfection of being that in this respect the least fly or *mite* is a more noble being than a star. — BISHOP ROBERT SOUTH.

6. The melancholy days have come, the saddest of the year,
   Of wailing winds, and naked woods, and meadows brown and *sere*. — WILLIAM CULLEN BRYANT.

7. Cherish veins of good humor and *sear* up those of ill.
   SIR WILLIAM TEMPLE.

8. I will not play the *seer*. — HENRY WADSWORTH LONGFELLOW.

9. Autumn *sears* not like grief,
   Nor kills such lovely flowers. — HENRY NEELEY.

LESSON 160.

Months.

1. Copy carefully. 2. Write from dictation, or from memory.

1. January gray is here. — Percy Bysshe Shelley.

2.   Come when the rains
Have glazed the snow and clothed the trees with ice,
While the slant sun of February pours
Into the bowers a flood of light.
                    — William Cullen Bryant.

3. Ah, March! we know thou art
Kind-hearted, spite of ugly looks and threats,
And, out of sight, art nursing April's violets.
                    — Helen Hunt Jackson.

4. A gush of bird-song, a patter of dew,
A cloud, and a rainbow's warning,
Suddenly sunshine and perfect blue, —
An April day in the morning.
                    Harriet Prescott Spofford.

5. When April steps aside for May,
Like diamonds all the rain-drops glisten;
Fresh violets open every day:
To some new bird each hour we listen. — Lucy Larcom.

6. And what is so rare as a day in June?
Then, if ever, come perfect days;
Then Heaven tries earth if it be in tune,
And over it softly her warm ear lays.
                    — James Russell Lowell.

LESSON 161.

Months.

1. Copy carefully.   2. Write from dictation, or from memory.

1. I remember, I remember,
   How my childhood flitted by, —
   The mirth of its December,
   The warmth of its July. — WINTHROP M. PRAED.

2. And August came the fainting year to mend
   With fruit and grain. — WILLIAM MORRIS.

3. The morrow was a bright September morn;
   The earth was beautiful as if new-born;
   There was that nameless splendor everywhere,
   That wild exhilaration in the air.
   — HENRY WADSWORTH LONGFELLOW.

4. October turned my maple's leaves to gold;
   The most are gone now; here and there one lingers;
   Soon these will slip from out the twig's weak hold.
   — THOMAS BAILEY ALDRICH.

5. No shade, no shine, no butterflies, no bees,
   No fruits, no flowers, no leaves, no birds,
      November! — THOMAS HOOD.

6. The sun that brief December day
   Rose cheerless over hills of gray,
   And, darkly circled, gave at noon
   A sadder light than waning moon.
   — JOHN GREENLEAF WHITTIER.

LESSON 162.

Some words pronounced alike.

1. Copy carefully. 2. Write from dictation. 3. Use the italicized words in sentences of your own.

1. What though care killed a cat, thou hast mettle enough in thee to *kill* care. — WILLIAM SHAKESPEARE.

2. Which is as hateful to me as the *reek* of a lime*kiln*. — WILLIAM SHAKESPEARE.

3. On me let death *wreak* all his rage. — JOHN MILTON.

4. In the coldness and the darkness all through the long night-time,
My grated casement whitened with autumn's early *rime*. — JOHN GREENLEAF WHITTIER.

5.   I have every good
For thee wished many a time,
Both sad and in a cheerful mood,
But never yet in *rhyme*. — WILLIAM COWPER.

6. Lament in *rhyme*, lament in prose,
With salt tears trickling down your nose.
                                 ROBERT BURNS.

7. *Rome, Rome*, thou art no more
As thou hast been!
On thy seven hills of yore
Thou sat'st a queen. — FELICIA D. HEMANS.

8. How much a dunce that has been sent to *roam*
Excels a dunce that has been kept at home.
                                   WILLIAM COWPER.

LESSON 163.

Some words pronounced alike.

1. Copy carefully. 2. Write from dictation. 3. Use the italicized words in sentences of your own.

1. For her griefs, so lively *shown*,
   Made me think upon mine own. — WILLIAM SHAKESPEARE.

2. The moon arose: she *shone* upon the lake,
   Which lay one smooth expanse of silver light.
   — ROBERT SOUTHEY.

3. The summer grains were harvested; the stubble fields lay dry,
   Where June winds rolled, in light and shade, the pale-green waves of *rye*.
   JOHN GREENLEAF WHITTIER.

4.   One of those
   With fair black eyes and hair, and a *wry* nose.
   BEN JONSON.

5. And then her hands she wildly *wrung*,
   And then she wept, and then she sung.
   — SIR WALTER SCOTT.

6. Harmonious concert *rung* in every part,
   While simple melody pour'd moving on the heart.
   ROBERT BURNS.

7. Mounts the *stile* with ease, or leaps the fence.
   WILLIAM COWPER.

8.   Whose large *style*
   Agrees not with the leanness of his purse.
   WILLIAM SHAKESPEARE.

LESSON 164.

Some words pronounced alike.

1. Copy carefully.   2. Write from dictation.   3. Use the italicized words in sentences of your own.

1. The trenchant blade, Toledo trusty,
   For want of fighting was grown rusty,
   And ate into itself for lack
   Of somebody to *hew* and hack. — SAMUEL BUTLER.

2. 'Tis distance lends enchantment to the view,
   And robes the mountain in its azure *hue*.
   THOMAS CAMPBELL.

3. That's a valiant *flea* that dare eat his breakfast on the lip of a lion. — WILLIAM SHAKESPEARE.

4. The wicked *flee* when no man pursueth: but the righteous are bold as a lion. — BIBLE.

5. In song he never had his *peer*. — JOHN DRYDEN.

6. Have raised you high as talents can ascend,
   Made you a *Peer*, but spoiled you for a friend.
   WILLIAM COWPER.

7. How wistfully would I wander about the *pier* heads in fine weather, and watch the parting ships!
   — WASHINGTON IRVING.

8. Is not to-day enough? Why do I *peer*
   Into the darkness of the day to come?
   Is not to-morrow even as yesterday?
   — PERCY BYSSHE SHELLEY.

LESSON 165.

Some words pronounced alike.

1. Copy carefully. 2. Write from dictation. 3. Use the italicized words in sentences of your own.

1. All the birds are *faint* with the hot sun. — JOHN KEATS.

2.   Oh, with what delight
Heard I that voice! and catch it now, though *faint*,
Far off and *faint*, and melting into air.
                — WILLIAM WORDSWORTH.

3.   Oh, stay! it was a *feint;*
She had no vision, and she heard no voice.
I said it but to awe thee. — PERCY BYSSHE SHELLEY.

4. And the sun looked over the mountain's brim,
And *straight* was a path of gold for him.
                ROBERT BROWNING.

5. Thus men go wrong with an ingenious skill,
Bend the *straight* rule to their own crooked will.
                — WILLIAM COWPER.

6. *Strait* is the gate, and narrow is the way, which leadeth unto life, and few there be that find it. — BIBLE.

7. There, mildly dimpling, Ocean's cheek
Reflects the tints of many a *peak*.
                GEORGE GORDON, LORD BYRON.

8. Out of personal *pique* to those in service, he stands as a looker-on when the government is attacked.
                — JOSEPH ADDISON.

LESSON 166.

A useful prefix.

in means *not;* as, *in*direct, *not* direct.

In words of Latin origin it regularly becomes *il-* before *l*, *ir-* before *r*, and *im-* before a labial: as, *b, m, p*.

1. Copy carefully.   2. Write from dictation.

1. *Inconstant* as the beams that play
On rippling waters in an April day. — WILLIAM COWPER.

2. I can get no remedy against this consumption of the purse: borrowing only lingers and lingers it out, but the disease is *incurable*.
WILLIAM SHAKESPEARE.

3. The *irregular*, the *illimitable*, and the luxuriant, have their appropriate force. — THOMAS DE QUINCEY.

4. An *irresistible* law of nature impels us to seek happiness. — WILLIAM MASON.

5. It is not a lucky word, this same *impossible;* no good comes of those that have it so often in their mouth. — THOMAS CARLYLE.

6. Boundless, endless, and sublime,
The image of eternity, the throne
Of the *invisible*. — GEORGE GORDON, LORD BYRON.

7. We are all tattooed in our cradles with the beliefs of our tribe; the record may seem superficial, but it is *indelible*. — OLIVER WENDELL HOLMES.

8. How idle a boast, after all, is the *immortality* of a name! — WASHINGTON IRVING.

LESSON 167.

Some words pronounced nearly alike.

1. Copy carefully. 2. Write from dictation. 3. Use the italicized words in sentences of your own. 4. Distinguish carefully any differences in the sounds of words nearly alike.

1. These are the tales, or new or old,
   In *idle* moments idly told.
   —HENRY WADSWORTH LONGFELLOW.

2. As *idle* as a painted ship upon a painted ocean.
   —SAMUEL TAYLOR COLERIDGE.

3. Content to be allowed at last
   To sing his *Idyl* of the Past.
   —HENRY WADSWORTH LONGFELLOW.

4. The *idol* of to-day pushes the hero of yesterday out of our recollection; and will, in turn, be supplanted by his successor of to-morrow.
   —WASHINGTON IRVING.

5. There by the door a hoary-headed sire
   Touched with his withered hand an ancient *lyre*.
   WILLIAM WORDSWORTH.

6. He was, in fact, the greatest *liar* I had met with then, or since. —CHARLES LAMB.

7. A pun is not bound by the laws which limit nicer wit. It is a *pistol* let off at the ear; not a feath r to tickle the intellect. —CHARLES LAMB.

8. Who cares how many stamens or *pistils* that little brown flower, which comes out before the leaf, may have to classify it by?
   —OLIVER WENDELL HOLMES.

LESSON 168.

Some words pronounced nearly alike.

1. Copy carefully. 2. Write from dictation. 3. Use the italicized words in sentences of your own. 4. Distinguish carefully the sounds of words nearly alike.

1. See what a lovely shell,
   Small and pure as a pearl,
   Made so fairly well
   With delicate spire and *whorl!* — ALFRED TENNYSON.

2. They *whirl* in narrow circling trails,
   Like kittens playing with their tails.
   — JOHANN W. GOETHE.

3. Beneath a summer sky
   From *flower* to *flower* let him fly.
   — WILLIAM WORDSWORTH.

4. For if the *flour* be fresh and sound,
   And if the bread be light and sweet,
   Who careth in what mill 'twas ground?
   — HENRY WADSWORTH LONGFELLOW.

5. The murmuring *surge*,
   That on the unnumber'd idle pebbles chafes.
   WILLIAM SHAKESPEARE.

6. And the smile and the tear, and the song and the dirge,
   Still follow each other like *surge* upon *surge*.
   — WILLIAM KNOX.

7. Thou *serge*, nay, thou buckram lord!
   — WILLIAM SHAKESPEARE.

LESSON 169.

Some words pronounced nearly alike.

1. Copy carefully. 2. Write from dictation. 3. Use the italicized words in sentences of your own. 4. Distinguish carefully the sounds of words nearly alike.

1. Ye *holy* walls that still sublime,
   Resist the crumbling touch of time. —Robert Burns.

2. And yet I know enough
   Not to be *wholly* ignorant. —Percy Bysshe Shelley.

3. Swift o'er the rolling pebbles, down the hills
   Louder and louder *purl* the falling rills.
   —Alexander Pope.

4. This rhyme is like the fair *pearl* necklace of the queen,
   That burst in dancing and the *pearls* were spilt.
   Alfred Tennyson.

5. In Russia, at the present moment, the aristocracy are dictated to by their emperor much as they themselves dictate to their *serfs*.
   — Herbert Spencer.

6. Light as the foamy *surf*,
   That the wind severs from the broken wave.
   —William Cowper.

7. 'Tis curiosity — who hath not felt
   Its spirit, and before its *altar* knelt?
   —Charles Sprague.

8. If he were
   To be made honest by an act of parliament,
   I should not *alter* in my faith of him. —Ben Jonson.

LESSON 170.

A useful prefix.

inter means *between*, as, *inter*line, to write or insert *between* the lines.

1. Copy carefully. 2. Write from dictation.

1. Then, rising with Aurora's light,
   The Muse invoked, sit down to write;
   Blot out, correct, insert, refine,
   Enlarge, diminish, *interline*. — JONATHAN SWIFT.

2.   The forest told
   Of grassy paths and wood-lawns *interspersed*
   With overarching elms, and caverns cold,
   And violet banks where sweet dreams brood.
                                PERCY BYSSHE SHELLEY.

3.   I did laugh without *intermission*
   An hour by his dial. — WILLIAM SHAKESPEARE.

4.   Sweet *interchange*
   Of hill and valley, rivers, woods, and plains,
   Now land, now sea, and shores with forests crowned.
                                — JOHN MILTON.

5. Where even the motion of an Angel's wing
   Would *interrupt* the intense tranquillity
   Of silent hills, and more than silent sky.
                                — WILLIAM WORDSWORTH.

6. Fresh woodbines climb and *interlace*,
   And keep the loosened stones in place.
                                — HENRY WADSWORTH LONGFELLOW.

LESSON 171.

Some words pronounced nearly alike.

1. Copy carefully. 2. Write from dictation. 3. Use the italicized words in sentences of your own. 4. Distinguish carefully the sound of words nearly alike.

1. King of England shalt thou be proclaimed
   In every *borough*. — WILLIAM SHAKESPEARE.

2. And on the lawn — within its turfy mound —
   The rabbit made its *burrow*. — THOMAS HOOD.

3. *Cannon* to right of them,
   Cannon to left of them,
   Cannon in front of them,
   Volley'd and thunder'd. — ALFRED TENNYSON.

4. It is a *canon* of philosophy not to seek for unknown causes when known causes sufficiently explain the event. — GAIL HAMILTON.

5. Labor in this country is independent and proud. It has not to ask the patronage of *capital*, but *capital* solicits the aid of labor. — DANIEL WEBSTER.

6. Such London is, by taste and wealth proclaimed
   The fairest *capital* of all the world. — WILLIAM COWPER.

7. Talking French to Miss Pinkerton was *capital* fun.
   — WILLIAM MAKEPEACE THACKERAY.

8. There the *capitol* thou seest
   Above the rest lifting his stately head. — JOHN MILTON.

LESSON 172.

Some words pronounced alike.

1. Copy carefully. 2. Write from dictation. 3. Use the italicized words in sentences of your own.

1. For ere that steep *ascent* was won,
   High in his pathway hung the sun.
   — Sir Walter Scott.

2. The vows to which her lips had sworn *assent*.
   — Percy Bysshe Shelley.

3. The ship is decked out in all her *canvas*, every sail swelled and careering gayly over the curling waves. — Washington Irving.

4. No previous *canvass* was made for me.
   — Edmund Burke.

5. In all governments truly republican, men are nothing — *principle* is everything — Daniel Webster.

6. Can you remember any of the *principal* evils that he laid to the charge of women? There were none *principal*; they were all like one another as half-pence are. — William Shakespeare.

7. There's none ever fear'd that the truth should be heard,
   But they whom the truth would *indict*.
   — Robert Burns.

8. Robert Burns has *indited* many songs that slip into the heart. — John Wilson.

LESSON 173.

Some words pronounced alike.

1. Copy carefully. 2. Write from dictation. 3. Use the italicized words in sentences of your own.

1. Now Nature hangs her *mantle* green
    On every blooming tree,
   And spreads her sheets of daisies white
    Out o'er the grassy lea. — ROBERT BURNS.

2. Mock oranges and conch shells decorated the *mantelpiece*; and strings of various-colored birds' eggs were suspended above it.
   — WASHINGTON IRVING.

3. Startling with *martial* sounds each rude recess,
   Where the deep echo slept in loneliness.
   FELICIA D. HEMANS.

4. Reason becomes the *marshal* to my will
   And leads me. — WILLIAM SHAKESPEARE.

5. He sets the bright procession on its way,
   And *marshals* all the order of the year.
   WILLIAM COWPER.

6. Then come the wild *weather*, come sleet or come snow,
   We will stand by each other, however it blow.
   — SIMON DACH.

7. My *wether's* bell rings doleful knell.
   WILLIAM SHAKESPEARE.

LESSON 174.

Some words pronounced nearly alike.

1. Copy carefully. 2. Write from dictation. 3. Use the italicized words in sentences of your own. 4. Distinguish carefully any differences in the sounds of words nearly alike.

1.   As brown in hue
As hazel nuts and sweeter than the *kernels*.
— WILLIAM SHAKESPEARE.

2. My honored *colonel*, deep I feel
Your interest in the poet's weal. — ROBERT BURNS.

3. O the dreary, dreary moorland! O the *barren, barren* shore! — ALFRED TENNYSON.

4. The flower among our *barons* bold. — ROBERT BURNS.

5.   Here's the note
How much your chain weighs to the utmost *carat*.
WILLIAM SHAKESPEARE.

6. And when his juicy salads failed,
Sliced *carrot* pleased him well. — WILLIAM COWPER.

7. Oh, sweet is thy *current* by town and by tower,
The green sunny vale and the dark linden bower!
— HORACE WALLACE.

8. So coin grows smooth, in traffic *current* passed,
Till Cæsar's image is effaced at last. — WILLIAM COWPER.

9.   The *currant* must escape
Though her small clusters imitate the grape.
NAHUM TATE.

LESSON 175.

A useful prefix.

sub means *under;* as, *sub*scribe, to write *under.* In words from the Latin it is regularly *suc-* before *c*, *suf-* before *f*, *sug-* before *g*, and *sup-* before *p*; *sum-* before *m*, and *sur-* before *r* occur in a few instances.

1. Copy carefully.   2. Write from dictation.

1. Was never *subject* longed to be a king,
   As I do long and wish to be a *subject.*
   — WILLIAM SHAKESPEARE.

2. Most people would *succeed* in small things if they were not troubled with great ambition.
   — HENRY WADSWORTH LONGFELLOW.

3. Who breathes, must *suffer;* and who thinks, must mourn. — MATTHEW PRIOR.

4. They'll take *suggestion* as a cat laps milk.
   WILLIAM SHAKESPEARE.

5. The sun was set, and Vesper to *supply*
   His absent beams had lighted up the sky.
   — JOHN DRYDEN.

6. Fine manners need the *support* of fine manners in others. — RALPH WALDO EMERSON.

7. But forth one wavelet, then another, curled,
   Till the whole sunrise, not to be *suppressed,*
   Rose, reddened, and its seething breast
   Flickered in bounds, grew gold, then overflowed the world. — ROBERT BROWNING.

LESSON 176.

Some words pronounced nearly alike.

1. Copy carefully. 2. Write from dictation. 3. Use the italicized words in sentences of your own. 4. Distinguish carefully sounds of words nearly alike.

1. A man without religion is like a horse without a
    bridle. — ROBERT BURTON.

2. Bell, thou soundest merrily,
   When the *bridal* party
   To the church doth hie!
   — HENRY WADSWORTH LONGFELLOW.

3. But 'tis done — all words are idle —
   Words from me are vainer still;
   But the thoughts we cannot *bridle*
   Force their way without the will.
   — GEORGE GORDON, LORD BYRON.

4. Raised by the mole, the *miner* of the soil.
   — WILLIAM COWPER.

5. Men's great actions are performed in *minor* struggles.
   — VICTOR HUGO.

6. Tell her, if you will, that sorrow
   Need not come in vain;
   Tell her that the *lesson* taught her
   Far outweighs the pain. — ADELAIDE A. PROCTER.

7. In proportion as the years both *lessen* and shorten, I set more count upon their periods, and would fain lay my ineffectual finger upon the spoke of the great wheel. — CHARLES LAMB.

LESSON 177.

Some words pronounced nearly alike.

1. Copy carefully. 2. Write from dictation. 3. Use the italicized words in sentences of your own. 4. Distinguish carefully sounds of words nearly alike.

1. Jails and state prisons are the *complement* of schools: so many less as you have of the latter, so many more you must have of the former.
— HORACE MANN.

2. To be trusted is a greater *compliment* than to be loved. — GEORGE MACDONALD.

3. I had thought I had had men of some understanding
And wisdom of my *council;* but I find none.
WILLIAM SHAKESPEARE.

4. No man will take *counsel*, but every man will take money: therefore money is better than *counsel*.
— JONATHAN SWIFT.

5. And what is more melancholy than the old apple trees that linger about the spot where once stood a homestead, but where there is now only a ruined chimney rising out of a grassy and weed-grown *cellar?* — NATHANIEL HAWTHORNE.

6. To things of sale a *seller's* praise belongs.
WILLIAM SHAKESPEARE.

7. Traces made of the smallest spider's web,
The *collars* of the moonshine's watery beams.
— WILLIAM SHAKESPEARE.

8. He is rash and very sudden in *choler*, and haply may strike at you. — WILLIAM SHAKESPEARE.

LESSON 178.

Some words pronounced nearly alike.

1. Copy carefully. 2. Write from dictation. 3. Use the italicized words in sentences of your own. 4. Distinguish carefully sounds of words nearly alike.

1. Tender handed stroke a nettle,
   And it stings you for your pains;
   Grasp it like a man of *mettle*,
   And it soft as silk remains. — AARON HILL.

2. I weigh the man, not his title; 'tis not the king's stamp can make the *metal* better or heavier.
   — WILLIAM WYCHERLY.

3. And did he not, in his protectorship,
   Levy great sums of money through the realm?
   WILLIAM SHAKESPEARE.

4. No more we see his *levee* door
   Philosophers and Poets pour. — ROBERT BURNS.

5. Nearing New Orleans, the country became perfectly level, and from the embankments or *levees* we could see the great river winding on for miles.
   — JOHN JAMES AUDUBON.

6. We pass a gulf in which the willows dip
   Their *pendent* boughs, stooping as if to drink.
   — WILLIAM COWPER.

7. Birds had found their way into the chapel, and built their nests among its friezes and *pendants*.
   WASHINGTON IRVING.

Pendent, an adjective. *Pendant*, a noun.

LESSON 179.

Verbal distinctions.

1. Copy carefully. 2. Write from dictation. 3. Use the italicized words in sentences of your own.

1. Thanks, gentlemen. I heartily *accept*
   This token.—PERCY BYSSHE SHELLEY.

2. The river lay motionless and glassy, *except* that here and there a gentle undulation moved and prolonged the blue shadow of the distant mountain.—WASHINGTON IRVING.

3. Many receive *advice*, only the wise profit by it.
   —PUBLIUS SYRUS.

4. One can *advise* comfortably from a safe port.
   —JOHANN C. F. SCHILLER.

5. Are there not little chapters in everybody's life that seem to be nothing, and yet *affect* all the rest of the history?
   —WILLIAM MAKEPEACE THACKERAY.

6. Severity is allowable when gentleness has no *effect*.
   —PIERRE CORNEILLE.

7. How beautiful is youth! How bright it gleams
   With its *illusions*, aspirations, dreams!
   —HENRY WADSWORTH LONGFELLOW.

8. When the least *allusion* was made to matrimony, he would look at the landlady's daughter and wink with both sides of his face.
   —OLIVER WENDELL HOLMES.

LESSON 180.

Verbal distinctions.

1. Copy carefully. 2. Write from dictation. 3. Use the italicized words in sentences of your own.

1. If one so rude and of so mean condition
   May pass into the *presence* of a king.
   —WILLIAM SHAKESPEARE.

2. Whoever makes great *presents* expects great *presents* in return.—MARCUS V. MARTIAL.

3. Like a jewel-finder's fierce *assay*,
   Of the prize he dug from its mountain tomb.
   —ROBERT BROWNING.

4. She could write a little *essay* on any subject, exactly a slate long, beginning at the left-hand top of one side, and ending at the right-hand bottom of the other.—CHARLES DICKENS.

5. And, after many a vain *essay*
   To captivate the tempting prey,
   Gives him at length the lucky pat,
   And has him safe beneath his hat.—WILLIAM COWPER.

6. A gentle respect and *deference* which may be kept as the unbought grace of life.
   —WILLIAM MAKEPEACE THACKERAY.

7. She lived unknown, and few could know
   When Lucy ceased to be;
   But she is in her grave, and oh!
   The *difference* to me!—WILLIAM WORDSWORTH.

LESSON 181.

Verbal distinctions.

1. Copy carefully.   2. Write from dictation.   3. Use the italicized words in sentences of your own.

1. Still to ourselves in every place consigned,
   Our own *felicity* we make or find. — Oliver Goldsmith.

2. The reign of Elizabeth was the age of learned ladies who read and wrote Greek with surprising *facility*. — Maximilian Schele de Vere.

3.   Ivy clasped
   The *fissured* stones with its entwining arms.
                         Percy Bysshe Shelley.

4. And to the *fisher's* chorus-note,
   Soft moves the dipping oar. — Joanna Baillie.

5. We have room and hospitality for *emigrants* who come to our shores to better their condition by the adoption of our citizenship.
                     — Chauncey Mitchell Depew.

6. The *immigrant*, on arriving, found himself a stranger in a strange land, far from friends.
                         — Ulysses S. Grant.

7. One might have mistaken him for the *genius* of famine descending upon the earth, or some scarecrow eloped from a cornfield.
                         — Washington Irving.

8. *Genius* and its rewards are briefly told:
   A liberal nature and a niggard doom,
   A difficult journey to a splendid tomb. — John Forster.

LESSON 182.

Verbal distinctions.

1. Copy carefully.   2. Write from dictation.   3. Use the italicized words in sentences of your own.

1. And in thy gentle speech, a *prophecy*
   Is whispered. — PERCY BYSSHE SHELLEY.

2. Always *prophesy* good fortune, unless there is an absolute impossibility of its fulfillment.
   — EDWARD BULWER, EARL LYTTON.

3.   For a moment think
   What meagre *profits* spread from pen and ink!
   GEORGE GORDON, LORD BYRON.

4. I shall always consider the best guesser the best *prophet*. — CICERO.

5.   A *sculptor* wields
   The chisel, and the stricken marble grows
   To beauty. — WILLIAM CULLEN BRYANT.

6. What *sculpture* is to a block of marble, education is to a human soul. — JOSEPH ADDISON.

7. We have strict *statutes* and most biting laws.
   — WILLIAM SHAKESPEARE.

8.   He's of *stature* somewhat low —
   Your hero always should be tall, you know.
   — CHARLES CHURCHILL.

9. History fades into fable; fact becomes clouded with doubt and controversy; the inscription moulders from the tablet; the *statue* falls from the pedestal. — WASHINGTON IRVING.

LESSON 183.

Verbal distinctions.

1. Copy carefully.   2. Write from dictation.   3. Use the italicized words in sentences of your own.

1.   The fiddle screams
Plaintive and piteous, as if it wept and wailed
Its wasted tones. — WILLIAM COWPER.

2. I say I rather think — but don't let that influence you — I rather think the *plaintiff* is the man.
— CHARLES DICKENS.

3. I remember a tall *poplar* of monumental proportions and aspect, a vast pillar of glassy green.
OLIVER WENDELL HOLMES.

4. On my once letting slip at table that I was not fond of a certain *popular* dish, he begged me at any rate not to say so, for the world would think me mad. — CHARLES LAMB.

5. Behold a gorgeous palace that amid
Yon *populous* city rears its thousand towers.
— PERCY BYSSHE SHELLEY.

6. A virtuous *populace* may rise the while,
And stand a wall of fire around their much-loved isle.
OLIVER GOLDSMITH.

7. The hoary morns *precede* the sunny days.
— ROBERT BURNS.

8. Too careless often as our years *proceed*,
What friends we sort with, or what books we read.
— WILLIAM COWPER.

LESSON 184.

Verbal distinctions.

1. Copy carefully. 2. Write from dictation. 3. Use the italicized words in sentences of your own.

1. The long habitation of a powerful and *ingenious* race has turned every rood of land to its best use.
— RALPH WALDO EMERSON.

2. What a pity to think that these fine *ingenuous* lads in a few years will all be changed into frivolous members of Parliament! — CHARLES LAMB.

3. The *lightning* now
Is tangled in tremulous skeins of rain.
— THOMAS BAILEY ALDRICH.

4. Man is a packhorse,
You may brighten his path by *lightening* his load.

5. The scene had lent
To the dark water's breast
Its every leaf and *lineament*
With more than truth expressed.
— PERCY BYSSHE SHELLEY.

6. There is no *liniment* for a broken heart.

7. It is pleasant to hear him discourse of *patience* — extolling it as the truest wisdom — and to see him during the last seven minutes that his dinner is getting ready. — CHARLES LAMB.

8. The doctor had few *patients*, no *patience* had his wife.

LESSON 185.

Verbal distinctions.

1. Copy carefully. 2. Write from dictation. 3. Use the italicized words in sentences of your own.

1. Her presence of mind is equal to the most pressing trials of life, but will sometimes *desert* her upon trifling occasions. — CHARLES LAMB.

2. Use every man after his *desert*, and who should 'scape whipping? — WILLIAM SHAKESPEARE.

3. O see where wide the golden sunlight flows —
The barren *desert* blossoms as the rose!
       RICHARD WATSON GILDER.

4. "Please your honor," quoth the peasant,
"This same *dessert* is not so pleasant;
Give me again my hollow tree,
A crust of bread, and liberty." — ALEXANDER POPE.

5. Tricks and turns that fancy may *devise*,
Are far too mean for Him that rules the skies.
       WILLIAM COWPER.

6. Courage, the highest gift, that scorns to bend
To mean *devices* for a sordid end. — GEORGE FARQUHAR.

7. Life in its large *extent* is scarce a span.
      — CHARLES COTTON.

8. I must bid adieu also to that poor temple of my childhood, to me more sacred at this moment than perhaps the biggest cathedral then *extant* could have been. — THOMAS CARLYLE.

LESSON 186.

Verbal distinctions.

1. Copy carefully. 2. Write from dictation. 3. Use the italicized words in sentences of your own.

1.   Melancholy
Is not, as you conceive, indisposition
Of body, but the mind's *disease*. — JOHN FORD.

2. So the people ceased to honor him during his lifetime, and quietly consigned him to forgetfulness after his *decease*. — NATHANIEL HAWTHORNE.

3.   Weariness
Can snore upon the flint, when resty sloth
Finds the down *pillow* hard. — WILLIAM SHAKESPEARE.

4. Yet all how beautiful! *pillars* of pearl
Propping the cliffs above. — WILLIAM HENRY BURLEIGH.

5. Habits that give them an *insight* into the nature of labor, and inspire within them a genuine sympathy with those whose lot it is to labor.
    — JOSIAH GILBERT HOLLAND.

6. And each *incited* each to noble deeds.
    — ALFRED TENNYSON.

7. Where the swift sun yet paused in his *descent*
Among the many-folded hills. — PERCY BYSSHE SHELLEY.

8. The art of gently saying strong things, or of insinuating my *dissent*, instead of uttering it right out at the risk of offence. — THOMAS CARLYLE.

To avoid fine, this book should be returned on
or before the date last stamped below